TALKING
with GOD

TALKING
with GOD

Divine Conversations
That Transform Daily Life

ROBERT L. MILLET

DESERET
BOOK

SALT LAKE CITY, UTAH

Library of Congress Cataloging-in-Publication Data

Millet, Robert L.
  Talking with God : divine conversations that transform daily life / Robert L. Millet.
    p. cm.
  Includes bibliographical references and index.
  ISBN 978-1-60641-654-9 (hardbound : alk. paper)
  1. Prayer—The Church of Jesus Christ of Latter-day Saints. 2. The Church of Jesus Christ of Latter-day Saints—Doctrines. 3. Mormon Church—Doctrines. I. Title.
  BV210.3.M55 2010
  248.3'2—dc22   2010001300

Printed in the United States of America
Edwards Brothers Incorporated, Ann Arbor, MI

10 9 8 7 6 5 4 3 2

Men and women of integrity, character, and purpose have ever recognized a power higher than themselves and have sought through prayer to be guided by such power. Such has it ever been. So shall it ever be.

—PRESIDENT THOMAS S. MONSON

CONTENTS

CONTENTS

DID YOU THINK TO PRAY?

Not long ago I received word that my beloved Uncle Joseph in Baton Rouge had just passed away. He and his sweet wife, Gladys, who had departed this life six months earlier, were mainstays in my life of faith for more than a half century. Each time we gathered as a family in their home, I was thrilled for two reasons: first, we would be treated to Aunt Gladys's fantastic cooking; and second, after dinner we would inevitably have a gospel discussion, one in which both children and adults participated. Through the years I posed more than my share of questions about God, Christ, miracles, the purpose of life, the spirit world, and heaven and hell. Being a serious student of scripture, Uncle Joseph was always equal to the task of answering. Further, he was one who knew about the life and teachings of his Lord and Master and, most important, he knew the Lord. And we young people sitting at his feet knew that he knew. He had the words of Christ on his lips. We trusted him, and we loved him.

For years my immediate family was not much involved in the Church. My dad was a very moral and upright man, a person whose goodness and integrity were known far and wide, a fun father and one whom I loved and respected deeply. For some reason, however, we simply were not involved for a season in spiritual things. And it was Uncle Joseph and Aunt Gladys who nudged, poked, prodded, invited, enticed, and led us back into Church activity and into a stronger relationship with God. My uncle baptized both my mother and me, and he became a family hero of sorts.

As the decades rolled by, we stayed in touch, met together for several hours whenever my wife, Shauna, and I visited Louisiana, renewed treasured associations, reminisced, and spoke often of sacred things. Uncle Joseph worked for Standard Oil Company (later Exxon) for forty years, mowed his lawn, serviced his own cars, and remained healthy and robust until shortly before he left us.

Just two weeks before he died, my cousin Linda (his daughter) and I walked into his hospital room. She had been by his side day and night for some time, but I hadn't seen him in six months. I wasn't prepared for the scene: wires and tubes in his nose and mouth and an IV in his right arm. I found myself weak in the knees and a little wobbly. My beloved hero was staring death in the face. I gave him a priesthood blessing to the effect that the Almighty would grant peace and comfort to him and his family.

And so when the phone call did come, I was not surprised, but I was still struck by the harsh reality of the occasion, the seeming finality of it all, and the poignant realization that our sweet brotherhood had been interrupted for a season by this mysterious event we call death. After I hung up the phone, I immediately fell on my knees next to the hotel bed (I was attending a conference in Chicago at the time) and poured out my soul to the one Being who could understand perfectly just what I felt. I prayed. I thanked God for my uncle's significant contribution to this world, for his trust in and devotion to Deity, for his example of Christlike living. I told my Heavenly Father that I would miss my dear friend greatly and that I looked forward to the time when our family gatherings would be resumed in a day when we no longer saw through a glass darkly and no longer knew only in part (1 Corinthians 13:12). We enter this life as helpless infants, and likewise we leave it helplessly in the face of death. I ached inside. I longed to turn back the pages of time. I wanted, more than anything, to be by his side at the moment of his passing. I was helpless, naked in my lack of control over the situation, and so I did the only thing I knew to do—I prayed.

I believe in God. I rejoice in the privilege it is to talk of Christ, to converse reverently on his name and nature, to speak boldly of his mission and ministry, to declare with conviction his immortality and infinity. In short, there are few things I delight more in doing than speaking of the Most High. There is, however, one thing I do enjoy more, and that is speaking to him. We call that communication *prayer*. Regular and consistent and sincere and dedicated prayer is a sacred activity, one that transforms us into persons of purpose and of power, wholly surrendered to the mind and will of God and holy in our separation from the distractions of this world. President Thomas S. Monson has taught: "Men and women of integrity, character, and purpose have ever recognized a power higher than themselves and have sought through prayer to be guided by such power. Such has it ever been. So shall it ever be."[1]

Surely more miracles would be wrought if more of us took the time and exerted the energy to petition our God in behalf of a darkened world that is traveling headlong toward spiritual dissolution. As theologian John Stott suggested, "I sometimes wonder if the comparatively slow progress towards world peace, world equity and world evangelization is not due, more than anything else, to the prayerlessness of the people of God."[2]

We pray because we read that some of the greatest men and women in history turned heavenward when they needed clarity and conviction. We pray because the Lord and his prophets and apostles counsel us, in the strongest of terms, to request wisdom from God (James 1:5–6), to ask, to seek, to knock (Matthew 7:7), to persist and importune (Luke 11:5–8). We pray because we so often find ourselves up against the wall, uncertain and unsure where or to whom we should turn, confident that no human being has the answers to our personal struggles. It is not unimportant that the English word *prayer* comes from the Latin root *precarius*—yes, a cousin to our word *precarious*. We pray out of desperation; we don't know where else to turn.[3] We pray because a blessing has come into our lives, a heavenly gift that we definitely know did not come from friends, neighbors, and acquaintances; we feel driven to offer gratitude to an omniscient, omnipotent, and omniloving Father. We pray, not to change God's mind but rather to learn the will of God and then to align our own wills with his.

We pray because our mothers and fathers, grandmothers and grandfathers, taught us as little ones to close our day with "Now I lay me down to sleep." The words may have been simple, the deeper purposes for the action not wholly grasped at the time, but a pattern was established, a pattern of prayer that would serve us well as we moved into adulthood. We pray because somewhere along the road of Christian discipleship we learned by precept and example to rely wholly, to rely alone, upon the merits, mercy, and grace of the Lord Jesus Christ (2 Nephi 31:19; Moroni 6:4). We pray because we want to acknowledge God, because we desire to praise his Holy Son, and because we long to feel comforted and empowered by his Holy Spirit. In short, we pray because we have been commanded to do so, because we need to, because we want to. For the unconverted, prayer may seem a burden or at best a duty. But for the seasoned Saint, one who has begun to grow up in the Lord and mature in the gifts and fruit of the Spirit (1 Corinthians 12–14; Galatians 5:22–25), prayer is a blessed opportunity, a consummate privilege, a remarkable honor for a finite, fallen creature to be allowed and even commanded to communicate with an infinite, pure, and glorified Being.

Because prayer is such a vital element of growth and spiritual formation, Satan, the archenemy of God and goodness, will do all he can to hinder us from praying. He will work to convince us that we are too tired, too sophisticated, too rational, too preoccupied, too unworthy to pray. These are lies spawned by the father of lies. And even if we manage temporarily to break the pull of spiritual inertia, he will seek to dilute the effectiveness of our prayers by leading us cunningly to be content with mediocrity, shallowness, and routine in our prayers. "We need to win the battle of the prayer threshold," Professor Stott observed. "To help me persevere in prayer, I sometimes imagine a very high stone wall, with the living God on the other side of it. In this walled garden he is waiting for me to come to him. There is only one way into the garden—a tiny door. Outside that door stands the devil with a drawn sword, ready to stop me. It is at this point that we need to defeat the devil in the name of Christ. That is the battle of the threshold.

"I think there are many of us who give up praying before we have even tried to fight this battle. The best way to win, in my experience, is to claim the promises of Scripture, which the devil cannot undo."[4]

In other words, we need a strong dose of what Elder Robert D. Hales called "Christian courage."[5]

Through this book we will explore many dimensions of prayer. In a world that is dying under the weight of its own moral lethargy, we will speak often of attitudes and actions that lead to holy zeal and dynamic discipleship. In

a society where religion has become but another compart-
ment in compartmentalized lives, we will come to appreciate why the Danish philosopher Soren Kierkegaard taught
that "purity of heart is to will one thing."[6] That one thing
is life within the kingdom of God, a life where the pure
in heart come to see and know God (Matthew 5:8; D&C
97:16, 21). And finally, in a culture that has not yet banned
religion and the religious but has nonetheless marginalized
and trivialized them, we will come to understand how a
meaningful prayer life contributes immeasurably to our
capacity to "look to God and live" (Alma 37:47).

If indeed the quality of our lives is largely a product of
the kinds of associations we enjoy, then we may rest assured that a person who spends much time in prayer will
blossom in personality and rise above pettiness, littleness
of soul, and mortal jealousies and fears. Just as contact
with degrading influences affects us adversely, almost as
though the words and deeds of the depraved become a
part of us, so people who regularly call upon God, pour
out their soul in prayer, and yearn for genuine communion—such people cannot help but be elevated by that
association. As theologian Scot McKnight put it plainly,
"The proof of one's theology is in prayer."[7]

Some years ago I read Billy Graham's autobiography
and was deeply touched by these words: "Although I have
much to be grateful for as I look back over my life, I also
have many regrets. I have failed many times, and I would
do many things differently.

"For one thing, I would speak less and study more, and

7

I would spend more time with my family. . . . *I would also spend more time in spiritual nurture,* seeking to grow closer to God so I could become more like Christ. *I would spend more time in prayer,* not just for myself but for others. I would spend more time studying the Bible and meditating on its truth, not only for sermon preparation but to apply its message to my life."[8]

I knelt that cold February evening in Chicago when I learned of my beloved uncle's death and poured out my soul to a holy God. I spoke of my grief, of my feelings of aloneness, but also of my profound appreciation that a gracious Father in Heaven had chosen to orchestrate events in my life so that I had been tenderly tutored by a man of God, gently guided along the path to him who is indeed "the way, the truth, and the life" (John 14:6). That night I sought the Balm of Gilead. That night I pleaded to be lifted out of my sorrow. And that night I felt to sing praises to a loving Lord who has won the victory over death and brought us life and immortality (1 Corinthians 15:54–55, 57; 2 Timothy 1:10).

Is there any miracle of man's devising that can equal what takes place when a simple prayer penetrates the veil separating us from God? I think not. Is there any technological advance that can match the miracle that has been extended to us, the miracle of communion with the Infinite? Surely not. What a supernal witness that the day of miracles has not ceased. Thanks be to God for the privilege and miracle of prayer.

Chapter 1

PREPARATION FOR PRAYER

More than twenty years ago I stood before an audience of about twenty-five hundred people who had come to Education Week on the Brigham Young University campus to hear a presentation on the Atonement of Jesus Christ. It was the first of four lectures I had been invited to deliver on the topic. It had been a busy month for me, racing in and out of town on various assignments, squeezing in moments here and there in my university office, hoping to find a block of three or four hours in order to prepare, but it was a segment of precious time that never materialized. I had spoken on this significant topic many times, and although I had always felt inadequate and incapable of doing justice to the subject, nevertheless the scriptural texts and ideas were in my mind. Glancing that morning at my watch and discovering that it was eight o'clock (the lecture was to begin at eight thirty), I frantically jotted down a few ideas and rushed off to the Wilkinson Center Ballroom.

I stood up with all the confidence in the world, glanced at my flimsy notes, and plunged in. I followed my rough outline fairly closely, moving from point to point with relative ease, and I felt as though the ideas were coming out and going down well. The audience seemed interested, and hundreds of individuals were earnestly taking notes. I came to the last item on my list, read and discussed the relevant scriptural passages, and reached the point in my outline marked "Conclusion." It had been a pretty good presentation, I thought to myself. All I really needed was a sketchy outline, it seemed. This lengthy preparation stuff was overrated. Then I furtively glanced at the clock. Immediately I began to sweat profusely, to wiggle a bit behind the pulpit, and to acknowledge a sick feeling in my stomach. Why? The meeting was scheduled to end at 9:25 A.M., and it was now all of 9:00! The speakers had been given very specific instructions:

1. Begin on time. Do not take long to get into your subject.
2. Do not allow questions. The audience is too large.
3. Take the entire period. Do not let people out early, for the noise of exiting the rooms will disrupt the other classrooms or lecture halls.

Twenty-five minutes early! What in the world was I to do? I hemmed and hawed and flitted from one idea to the next, sensing the unease of the audience and recognizing their disappointment in the painful reality that their teacher had underprepared.

That has never happened to me since. I vowed that day that I would never, ever, underprepare. I would never try to wing it at the expense of those who come to the table hungry to be fed the pleasing word of God, the word that "healeth the wounded soul" (Jacob 2:8). The children of God deserve better. Rather, I have overprepared in that I have always organized much more material and many more ideas than I can possibly cover in an hour. I have prayed for divine guidance and sought to go where the Spirit led, to focus on those matters that seemed most pertinent at the moment.

Preparation precedes power, and not just in lessons and sermons. If you or I were granted the privilege to spend an hour with the president of the United States, the president of the Church, the pope, an apostle, or someone else for whom we have great respect, and we knew of the meeting ahead of time, I'm pretty certain we would not rush into the person's office and blather on and on about the first things that came to mind. Rather, we would have spent time prayerfully reflecting on the things of greatest worth, the questions and issues that might be raised, that would be most meaningful. We would want to be prepared.

And so it is with prayer. We should not expect to rush into the presence of Deity, mouth a few well-worn phrases, race away, and then feel satisfied with the marvelous spiritual experience we have just enjoyed. We prepare out of respect and love. We prepare because time is precious, and we want our limited moments to be taken up in weightier matters. We prepare so that we might be in a position to drink in all of the living water that a gracious Lord is willing to dispense.

May I share a few ideas? Many prefer to sit quietly and meditate reverently upon holy matters, to rid the mind of schedules and appointments and dates and clothes and portfolios, to set aside the elements of *time* in order to engage the things of *eternity*. Some, including me, find it especially helpful to read scripture and reflect deeply before beginning prayer, pondering not only upon the story or incident on the printed page but also on how it relates to me or how it might be applied to my own life.

I confess that I am drawn regularly to the Gospel and the Epistles of John, where such marvelous themes as the Word, rebirth, the Bread of Life, love and unity, and becoming the sons and daughters of God are highlighted. A pastor friend of mine is especially drawn to the Psalms, largely because many of the psalms are themselves prayers of praise, petition, contrition, and deliverance. I am fully persuaded that one of the grand keys to *individual* revelation and guidance is a regular immersion in *institutional* revelation, namely, holy scripture. As the apostle Paul wrote so descriptively, "All scripture is breathed out by God and profitable for teaching, for reproof, for correction, and for training in righteousness, that the man of God may be competent, equipped for every good work" (2 Timothy 3:16–17, English Standard Version). The language, logic, and love that derive from holy writ are superb preparation for communing with the Infinite.

One woman I know loves to sit quietly and listen to sacred or inspiring music to settle her soul and focus her mind before prayer. She often listens to classical music and some of the great hymns or anthems of worship, hymns that are drenched in the doctrine of Christ. Others, especially those of a younger generation, choose to listen to the melodies and lyrics of more contemporary gospel music. Whatever our choice of music, however, we must keep in mind that the "song of the heart" is a prayer itself (D&C 25:12), that we are in a sense praying through music before we pray in words.

Through the years I have found that hymns chase away the inner noise and transform my thoughts and feelings in such a way that I approach the Lord in prayer with a far more reverent and yearning disposition. For me, listening to or singing "I Stand All Amazed," "Come, Thou Fount of Every Blessing," "How Great Thou Art," "More Holiness Give Me," "Faith of Our Fathers," "How Firm a Foundation," or "I Know That My Redeemer Lives" changes me, rearranges me, and readies me for a celestial conversation.

Often when I have been required to engage weighty matters—to make difficult and demanding decisions—I have taken the time to grab my scriptures, hop in the car, and drive up the canyon to be alone and undistracted in the midst of God's glorious creations. Nature is spiritually therapeutic. I don't spend all of my time on my knees, although there is in fact much time for that. I sit and read for half an hour, take a walk, reflect on my concern, lift my voice heavenward, and find solace and delight in silence. Once, while on a tour of the British Isles, I chose not to take the day off for window shopping and purchasing souvenirs with the rest of the group but rather to walk half a mile from our bed and breakfast, climb the steep hills, and situate myself so that I could see a number of the small towns and villages within about twenty or thirty miles. There I spoke with God, expressed that I was in desperate need of wisdom concerning a priesthood matter—I was a stake president at the time and needed to call two new bishops—and pleaded for divine direction. I remember that it was while reading in the First Epistle of John that an impression found its way into my mind, an answer to my prayers that I had not considered at all but one that was a reassuring resolution.

Now, I don't believe we need to go to England or Rome or Jerusalem or Mecca or Salt Lake City to receive answers to our prayers, but I do believe that too often we seek the sacred in the midst of noise and confusion, when what we need most at the time is to get away, leave behind our troubles, forsake the radio and television, and escape into sweet simplicity and serenity. Jehovah counseled beautifully: "Be still, and know that I am God" (Psalm 46:10).

Growing up in Louisiana, I learned firsthand the absolute necessity to prepare for hurricanes. One of the earliest memories I have is of Hurricane Audrey in the 1950s and of the fear and anxiety that filled the hearts of my family and friends as the newscasters and weathermen spoke in ominous tones of the gradual movement of this monster toward the Gulf coast. We filled the bathtub with water for drinking. We boarded up the windows and screen porch and tied down everything outside the home that might be blown away or splintered by winds of 140 miles per hour. I remember driving with my grandfather to the grocery store to stock up on food, only to find the store completely empty—shelves upon shelves that had only hours before been filled with bread, milk, cereal, fruit, detergent, sugar, flour, and dog food were now completely empty. It was a creepy sight. One either prepares for a hurricane or one suffers the consequences, as witnessed in recent years by the tragic devastation wrought by Hurricane Katrina in New Orleans.

We must prepare here and now for what the scriptures call the "great and the terrible day of the Lord" (Joel 2:31), namely, the second coming of Christ in glory. We will either be, as Paul graphically described it, the children of light who have made proper preparations for that time, or we will be the children of darkness, who procrastinated the day of our repentance until it was everlastingly too late (1 Thessalonians 5:1–6; Helaman 13:38; Alma 13:27). We pray here and now to prepare for that which is to come, whether trials or tribulations or traumas, and we pray specifically to be ready for the return of the Son of Man, who will then reign for a thousand years as King of Kings and Lord of Lords (Revelation 17:14; 19:16). We are preparing now to meet God, and we can rest assured that to the extent we have prepared properly for prayer, have enjoyed sweet association with the Almighty in prayer, and have had our lives purified and enriched thereby, we will enjoy the smile of his sweet approbation.

Chapter 2

THE LORD'S PRAYER

In the middle of the majestic Sermon on the Mount, Matthew records the Savior's warnings against performing good deeds, fasting, and praying to be seen and heard by others—that is, doing the right things for the wrong reason. "Be not ye therefore like unto them [the heathen]: for your Father knoweth what things ye have need of, before ye ask him. After this manner therefore pray ye: Our Father which art in heaven, Hallowed be thy name. Thy kingdom come. Thy will be done in earth, as it is in heaven. Give us this day our daily bread. And forgive us our debts, as we forgive our debtors. And lead us not into temptation, but deliver us from evil: For thine is the kingdom, and the power, and the glory, for ever. Amen" (Matthew 6:8–13).

Here we have it, what the Christian world has come to know as the Lord's Prayer. Millions upon millions of Christians recite it regularly, a large number of them as a part of their religious worship. For some it is whispered in times of crisis or impending death. For others it is pronounced at any large gathering of disciples. For a surprising number it is the only prayer they ever utter. Christian scholar Dietrich Bonhoeffer observed that "Jesus told his disciples not only *how* to pray, but also *what* to pray. The Lord's Prayer is not merely the pattern prayer, it is the way Christians *must* pray. If they pray this prayer, God will certainly hear them. The Lord's Prayer is the quintessence of prayer. A disciple's prayer is founded on and circumscribed by it."[1]

Let's consider briefly each phrase of the Lord's Prayer.

"Our Father which art in heaven." We have been instructed to lift our voices and direct our thoughts to God, our Heavenly Father, in the name of the Son, by the power of the Holy Ghost. Our God has all power, knows all things, and by means of his Spirit is in and through and round about all things. We may approach him with faith—with total trust, complete confidence, and a ready reliance. He is as open to the prayer of a little child as he is to that of a lifelong believer, as eager to respond to the tender pleadings of a high school dropout as he is to attend to the eloquence of a university president. Any and every person can pray: There is no ceiling on the number of petitions God hears and grants, no limit on the quantity of requests that an infinite and eternal Being can hear and consider. Our God *is* God.

"Hallowed be thy name." To *hallow* is to honor, make holy, consecrate, purify, sanctify, and reverence. To hallow the name of God is to think of it as singular and unique,

to speak of it with reverential fear and trembling, to act upon it with solemnity and sobriety. No thinking person who truly believes in God would ever use the awesome name of God—be it Elohim or Jehovah or Jesus Christ—lightly or as an exclamation or, even worse, as a curse or profanity. Anciently the word *profane* was the opposite of holy and meant literally "outside the temple." We profane the name of Deity when we drag something holy through the mire of worldliness and remove it from its distinctively holy context.

"Thy kingdom come." A heartfelt request for divine powers to establish the kingdom of God on earth, this phrase is a plea for the spread of the gospel of Jesus Christ, the dissemination of diligence and discipleship, the growth of goodness in the earth. It is a yearning request that the name and work of Christ spread to every nation, tongue, and people, as well as a tempered desire that practical Christianity be exercised more fully in homes and families, neighborhoods, and communities. To enter the kingdom of God "is to see, seek, receive, and enter a new political and social and spiritual reality [Christ] calls the kingdom (or empire) of God, or the kingdom (or empire) of heaven." It is vital to understand that "in the kingdom of God, the ultimate authority is not Caesar but rather the Creator. And you find your identity—your citizenship—not in Rome but rather in a spiritual realm, in the presence of God."[2]

"Thy will be done in earth, as it is in heaven." The gospel of Jesus Christ—"the power of God unto salvation" (Romans 1:16)—is intended to do far more than to make

people better, although that in itself is a pretty fair accomplishment. The gospel is intended to regenerate individual human beings and renovate whole societies. It is to make of earth a heaven. To pray "thy will be done" is easy enough, or at least it is easy enough to say the words. But to truly mean it is another matter, with far more serious and long-range implications than we may realize. To pray with earnestness for God's will to be done may well prove inconvenient, unsettling to our self-centered world, and off-putting to those who want to "do their own thing" or "march to a different drummer." This is a call for us to align ourselves with the purposes of heaven. It entails first a serious spiritual search to come to know what God wants done and then a consecrated effort to comply happily. To come unto Christ is a choice; it is a choice to be changed.

"Give us this day our daily bread." It is neither inappropriate nor selfish to ask God to assist us in meeting our daily needs for shelter, clothing, and food. Such is, in fact, a healthy exercise in humility, an open acknowledgment that we simply cannot make it in this life alone. We must have help. And so we pray sincerely for gainful employment, for a steady income, for sufficient to meet our needs. As disciples of Jesus we do not pray for wealth, for truckloads of cash or silos of gold, but rather for enough to live comfortably. Nor do we become overly anxious about the future: the Supreme Being cares for the lilies of the field and the birds that fly above the earth; does he not concern himself even more with the crowning jewel of his

creation, his children? The Redeemer's charge was for his followers to seek first the kingdom of God, being assured that eventually "all these things shall be added unto you" (Matthew 6:25–33).

"And forgive us our debts, as we forgive our debtors." Here it seems the Master is speaking of our offenses against God, our provocations against God's children, in short, our sins. Because no one, save Jesus only, has ever walked earth's paths without sin—because "all have sinned, and come short of the glory of God" (Romans 3:23)—all are in need of pardoning mercy. No one is exempt. We cannot work off our spiritual debts, earn a remission of them, or barter for a right standing before God. We must confess our misdeeds to him who knows all things, plead and pray for the necessary broken heart and contrite spirit (Psalm 34:17; 51:17), and realize that every sin is a sin against God (Psalm 51:1–4). He pardons. He extends mercy. He forgives. And he has made it abundantly clear that if we withhold forgiveness from those who have sinned against us, he will withhold forgiveness from us (Matthew 18:21–35). We are in no position to judge others' motives; we simply do not have the data, the requisite glance into their hearts, to know whether they are worthy of our pardon. We have not been called to be God, only to follow his commandments, including the charge to forgive our brothers and sisters (D&C 64:9–10).

"And lead us not into temptation, but deliver us from evil." Through the centuries many have thought this plea to be an odd one, given that God never tempts any person

to do wrong (James 1:13). The New American Bible renders this passage as "do not subject us to the final test, but deliver us from the evil one." The English Standard Version offers this note on the verse: "The meaning here most likely carries the sense, 'Allow us to be spared from difficult circumstances that would tempt us to sin.'" And I love the simple and charming rendering in Christian scholar Eugene Peterson's *The Message:* "Keep us safe from ourselves and the Devil."[3] The Prophet Joseph's Inspired Translation has it simply, "Suffer us not to be led into temptation." Satan is an insomniac, and no mortal can match his phenomenal powers or resist his continuing and cunning urges and invitations to transgress the laws of God, unless that mortal is strengthened and empowered from on high. Faith in Christ provides for us an elevated perspective on life, and it is through having the distant view, the big picture, that we are enabled to dismiss Satan and disregard his enticements (see Alma 37:33).

"For thine is the kingdom, and the power, and the glory, for ever. Amen." Many New Testament manuscripts do not contain these words to close the Lord's Prayer, but in point of fact they are found in the Didache, a document that scholars date to the first century, one that contains Jesus' teachings to his apostles. Further, they are found in the Book of Mormon (3 Nephi 13:13). The words provide an elegant and inspiring way to complete the Lord's Prayer. We end in an attitude of praise, of humble acknowledgment of who we are and who God is.

Chapter 3

IN THE NAME
OF THE SON

There is a name that is above every name that is named on earth or in heaven. It is the name of the One sent to bring salvation, the name of the One who paid an infinite price to ransom us from Satan. It is the blessed name of Jesus Christ. "Wherefore God also hath highly exalted him, and given him a name which is above every name: that at the name of Jesus every knee should bow, of things in heaven, and things in earth, and things under the earth; and that every tongue should confess that Jesus Christ is Lord, to the glory of God the Father" (Philippians 2:9–11). "For this cause I bow my knees unto the Father of our Lord Jesus Christ," Paul wrote on another occasion, "of whom the whole family in heaven and earth is named" (Ephesians 3:14–15).

To fully appreciate what it means to do all things in the name of Jesus, including to pray in his name, we must grasp and acknowledge our spiritual plight. Because of the Fall of our first parents, physical death entered into the world. Mortality itself implies that each of us is born and that each of us will in time face death. In addition, because of the Fall, each of us suffers spiritual death, which is separation from the presence of God and alienation from things of righteousness (Alma 12:16; 42:9; Helaman 14:18). It is true that each of us is created in the image and likeness of God, but through the Fall that image has been marred. It must be reshaped. The natural man—unredeemed, unregenerate, and spiritually stillborn—must be resuscitated (Mosiah 3:19).

The natural man does not receive or perceive the things of the Spirit of God, for they appear foolish to him (1 Corinthians 2:14). He works against the plan of God, against his own best interests (Alma 41:10). "Fallen man is not simply an imperfect creature who needs improvement: he is a rebel who must lay down his arms."[1] Because of the Fall we are alienated from the family of God; in a very real sense, we are nameless and without family. To use the graphic language of the King James Version, we are "bastards, and not sons" (Hebrews 12:8), or "illegitimate and not sons" (New King James Version).

Consequently, we must be born again. We must, through spiritual transformation, be changed from a carnal and fallen state to a state of righteousness (Mosiah 27:24–26); we must be redeemed, purchased, bought back from Satan, to whom we have sold ourselves through sin (Isaiah 50:1). As John the Beloved explained, those who receive Christ are given the power to be called the sons and daughters of God (John 1:12; compare 1 John 3:1–2).

Those born of the Spirit reenter the family of God and take upon them the name of Christ, the only name by which salvation can come (Acts 4:12; Mosiah 3:17). They are expected to take upon them that holy name, to become Christians, followers of the Christ, in word and deed. They are expected to bear and wear that name with fidelity and devotion, so as never to bring disrespect upon their family name. They are counseled to remember who they are—and Whose they are—and to act accordingly.

Jesus is our Lord and Savior, our Redeemer from death and hell and endless torment. He is our Mediator with the Father, our Intercessor (1 Timothy 2:5–6). He pleads our cause in the courts of glory. God, through Christ, reconciles the world to himself (2 Corinthians 5:18–20). Accordingly, Jesus is our way to the Father (John 14:6). Jesus did what no human being was able to do, not the greatest prophet or the mightiest apostle: He kept the law of God perfectly and remained without sin (2 Corinthians 5:21; Hebrews 4:14–15; 1 Peter 2:21–22). He never took a moral detour. He never took a backward step. Thus in his unique position, by virtue of his holiness and merits, he is able to succor ("to run to help") those who find themselves burdened by sin and its consequences. And so it is that the Master taught his disciples to pray to the Father in the name of the Son (John 14:13; 15:16; Colossians 3:17; 3 Nephi 18:20).

While serving as dean of Religious Education at Brigham Young University, I was frequently required to leave town for extended periods to give speeches, attend academic or administrative conferences, and undertake fund-raising and interfaith activities. Before I left I would sit down with my two associate deans to cover any last-minute details and give them complete authority to operate in my absence. They knew full well that meant they could make decisions, interpret policies, and even sign my name when necessary. I had confidence in their skills, background, and judgment; they had my permission to act in my name. I may have been the principal, but they were my agents, authorized to speak for the dean and the office of the dean.

There is power in a name, particularly when that name opens doors, unlocks opportunities, and equips us to act and speak with authority. We have been instructed that when we act and speak in the name of our blessed Lord, we are entitled to come boldly unto the throne of grace to receive assistance and entrance in time of need (Hebrews 4:16; Moses 7:59).

This is not magic or voodoo or some occult practice. It is about the name of Jesus. It is about approaching our beneficent Father in prayer with humble confidence in the blood of the sinless Son of Man because of the unique status he enjoys with the Father (Alma 33:11, 16). It is as though the Savior had said to each of us, "Go to our Father in prayer and, by the way, use my name." The Savior's name carries spiritual clout, real moral authority in the universe. It is so much more than offering a prayer and quickly closing it in Jesus' name. It is a lesson worthy of sober reflection and meditation, a lesson that ought to stay fresh in our minds and hearts, a lesson that ought to affect how we pray, how intently we concentrate, how sincerely we plead, what words we use, and how devoutly we thank and ask and approach the God of all creation.

After the death and resurrection of Christ, and having been endowed with power from on high at Pentecost (Luke 24:49; Acts 1:4), the apostles went about proclaiming the "ministry of reconciliation" (2 Corinthians 5:18) with a spiritual dynamism, a boldness of soul, and a depth of understanding that was clearly lacking before the Lord's passion and his rise to glory from the Arimathean's tomb. Peter and John performed a notable miracle in healing the lame man at the temple gate called Beautiful (Acts 3:2–10). They were then taken before the Jewish leaders and questioned regarding the healing: "*By what power, or by what name,* have ye done this?" (Acts 4:7; emphasis added). Peter testified that it had been accomplished through the name of Jesus Christ, "whom ye crucified, whom God raised from the dead, even by him doth this [formerly lame] man stand here before you whole" (Acts 4:10). They taught Jesus Christ and him crucified, and they cared precious little about how this teaching was received by their detractors. Having ignored the Sanhedrin's strong warning that they were not to teach Christ in public any longer, Peter spoke with fearlessness: "We ought to obey God rather than men" (Acts 5:29).

Truly there is power in a name. The balance between, on the one hand, a healthy and righteous focus on Jesus Christ and the careful use of his beloved name, and on the other hand, the unhealthy, spiritually unstable, and vain repetition of his name, may not be easy to find, but it is important. The scriptures do not teach us to flaunt or multiply the name of our Lord in speech, sermons, or prayers, as though his holy name were some kind of a mantra. The key to fellowship with the Father and the Son (1 John 1:3) lies not in how many times we speak the name but rather in how reverently and intently we approach the throne of grace.

Chapter 4

IF GOD KNOWS ALL

On many occasions, as a priesthood leader, I sat and listened to a member of the Church confess a serious sin. The mood was sober, feelings were close to the surface, and the individual opposite me was humble and penitent. In many of those interviews the member of the Church manifested the requisite broken heart and contrite spirit of which the scriptures speak (Psalm 51:7; 3 Nephi 9:20; D&C 59:8).

After I had determined that the sin had been fully confessed, that the confessor was willing to do whatever was needed to bring about the promised miracle of forgiveness, I frequently asked, "Have you confessed your sin to your Heavenly Father?"

Invariably the person responded with a puzzled look, a lengthy hesitation and silence, and then, "What do you mean?"

"Well, you have confessed your transgression to the

Lord's servant, but have you confessed it to the Lord himself?"

The unspoken answer was generally no, but aloud it came in the form of "Why would I need to confess to God? He already knows about this, doesn't he?"

Such a question evidences a lack of understanding that all sins must, absolutely must, be confessed first and foremost to God the Eternal Father. Of course he has all knowledge. In the words of Jacob, son of Lehi, "O how great the holiness of our God! For he knoweth all things, and there is not anything save he knows it" (2 Nephi 9:20). He is indeed omniscient. There is not the slightest sliver of knowledge that he does not possess. As the Prophet Joseph Smith testified, if you and I did not understand that God knows all things, we "could not exercise faith in him for life and salvation."[1] Our God possesses all the attributes of godliness in perfection, as does his Son Jesus Christ, who received a fulness of the glory and power of the Father in the Resurrection (Matthew 28:18; D&C 93:16–17).[2]

But the issue isn't whether God knows all things, including our personal sins and misdeeds. The issue is whether I as a sinner have spoken to my Eternal Father about my sins, whether I have confessed to him, whether I have shared with him the nature of the sin and my feelings about what I have done. Have I counseled with him in prayer? Have I poured out my heart, expressed my own sorrow and disappointment and even anguish of soul? Have I acknowledged the seriousness of my behavior and my emotions? Have I committed to God that I will never be guilty of such conduct again?

As it is in repentance, so it is with prayer in general: Our Father knows all things, long before we ever discuss them with him. He knows what we are going to say, what we will ask for. He does not need for us to speak the words or feel the feelings. But *we* need to say the words, express the feelings, and ask for his divine help. It is spiritually therapeutic. It is the healthy and proper thing to do. We need to form our thoughts and feelings into words, and we need to hear those words. God knows all things, but we do not. He has an elevated perspective on life here and hereafter, but we do not. He knows the answers to all of the questions, but we do not. He knows perfectly what we must do to align ourselves with his mind and will, and he wants us to know these things as well. To do so we must approach him in prayer.

Now, this is not just a matter of seeing prayer as some form of catharsis, of feeling better because we are able to get the problem on the table and discuss it with someone. If that were the case, it would be just as efficacious, just as lifting and spiritually liberating, for us to share our deepest concerns—including our sins—with a roommate, best friend, or spouse. Such conversations might make us feel better emotionally, but they do not meet the deeper spiritual needs that appropriate dialogue with God provides. God, and God alone, forgives sins. God, and God alone, is the author of the plan of salvation, the great plan of happiness. God, and God alone, is worthy to receive our prayers, our heaven-sent petitions.

Clearly, prayer accomplishes more than confessing sin and dispensing information. Through prayer we learn to commune with Deity. Through prayer we learn to transcend personal whims and temporal attachments. Through prayer we ascend to a higher realm of consciousness and come to think and feel and perceive in entirely new ways. The apostle Paul pleaded with the Saints of his day not to be "conformed to this world: but be ye transformed by the renewing of your mind" (Romans 12:2) to such an extent that eventually it might be said, "we have the mind of Christ" (1 Corinthians 2:16).

If the quality of a person's life is determined largely by the kind of people with whom he or she associates regularly, then we should contemplate soberly for a moment what a supernal difference it makes to our quality of life, here and hereafter, if we have grown into a meaningful prayer life. As the Prophet Joseph learned in Liberty Jail, "God shall give unto you knowledge by his Holy Spirit, yea, by the unspeakable gift of the Holy Ghost," knowledge "that has not been revealed since the world was until now; which our forefathers have awaited with anxious expectation to be revealed in the last times" (D&C 121:26–27). Indeed, God is making known the mysteries of the universe to those who prepare themselves to receive. Prayer is our lifeline to divine knowledge and power.

Chapter 5

FAITH IN OUR PRAYERS

Some years ago an anti-Mormon organization placed forty thousand copies of a book on the doorsteps of people living in the Orem and Provo areas of Utah. The book was intended to warn those not of the LDS faith to avoid the Mormons and those within the faith to get out as quickly as they could. A little over a hundred pages into the book, the author, a former Latter-day Saint himself, spoke of the knock on the door that would inevitably come and of the two well-dressed young men or young women who would be waiting at the door to explain their message. The author pleaded with readers not to let the missionaries in. If, however, their sense of Christian charity overcame them and they let the young people in, then whatever they did, they must not listen to them. But if the missionaries were able to share their message before they could be stopped, the missionaries would eventually ask the person to pray about the message of Mormonism. The author warned his readers never, never to allow themselves to do such a thing. In fact, the writer added, a seeker after truth must never trust thoughts, feelings, and prayers when ascertaining the truthfulness of any message. There is only one thing that can be trusted, and that is the Holy Bible.

My first thought was, How can a person make any sense out of the Bible if he or she does not dare think, feel, or pray? The writer explained that because each of us is a fallen creature, a depraved man or woman who has not the power to discern what is right and what is wrong, we are lost forever unless a power outside and beyond us comes into our lives and leads us to the gospel path. What we think is good is actually bad. What we think is wrong will usually be right. Our thoughts are polluted. Our feelings are degraded. Our prayers are useless.

Whatever happened to the invitation to seek, to ask, to knock in order to receive blessings and guidance from God? (Matthew 7:7–8). What about the powerful invitation to ask God for wisdom, knowing that he is eager and willing to grant it? (James 1:5). Why even give us the Lord's Prayer as a pattern, an example, if in fact we are not safe in offering up our petitions to the heavens?

Nephi warned us that the evil spirit teaches a man not to pray, but the Spirit of God will always invite us to express our needs and wants to a loving Father (2 Nephi 32:8–9). It is in fact a diabolical and nefarious ploy to warn people not to pray, to frighten them into believing that we may not with confidence pray and receive answers. If only the pure in heart prayed, if only the spiritually refined lifted up their voices to God, if only those who have been purified of all sin importuned the heavens, this world would be even worse than it is now. The church of the Lamb of God, the body of Christ, is made up of men and women who are striving to bring their lives into conformity with the Savior's teachings, but they are still human, still finite, still unholy. Their desires are noble, but often their conduct falls below the divine standard. If we cannot feel good about praying, if we must constantly stew and fret about whether we will be deceived in prayer, we are of all people most miserable. And we are truly left without help.

I testify that you and I have every right to pray, every reason to trust our Eternal Father, every motivation to lean upon his Holy Son. Christ is the embodiment of perfect love, and perfect love casts out all fear (1 John 4:18; Moroni 8:16). Satan cannot overpower a man who prays earnestly. The evil one cannot come off conqueror of the woman who is found regularly on her knees. We can have faith in prayer. We have every reason to come boldly unto the throne of grace of him whose every word was true and every action was righteous (Hebrews 4:16), every reason to be not arrogant but confident. Faith is confidence. Faith is trust. Faith is reliance. We can rest assured that God will hear our prayers, that he will inform and inspire us as we seek him.

If I could not trust in the power of prayer to comfort my soul, to provide perspective in a world of confusion, to empower me with the word of God to "divide asunder

all the cunning and the snares and the wiles of the devil"
(Helaman 3:29)—if prayer were not an option, I would not
know where to turn or how to find sanity amidst the mad-
ness of a decaying culture. Prayer has been for me like an
oasis in the middle of a barren desert, a consulate within a
war zone. Thanks be to God that our prayers have meaning and that they are heard. Because I understand that my
soul's deepest yearnings are laid before the pleasing bar of
the almighty Elohim, I have the strength to pray without
ceasing, to pray always.

Chapter 6

ANSWERS TO PRAYER

Jesus revealed a marvelous truth, a consummate insight, when he explained: "I am the vine, ye are the branches: He that abideth in me, and I in him, the same bringeth forth much fruit: for without me ye can do nothing" (John 15:5). Truly we are nothing without our Lord and Savior. We are nothing without our God and Father. We are at best, as King Benjamin observed, "unprofitable servants" (Mosiah 2:21; compare Luke 17:10). Save there had been a plan of redemption, an atoning sacrifice, a means of recovery and renewal, even "all our righteousnesses are as filthy rags" (Isaiah 64:6). Such revelations are in no way intended to discourage us, to create within us feelings of futility; rather, it is important that we live and move and have our being clothed in a mantle of humility. To be humble is to see things as they really are, to see ourselves as we really are, to see God as he really is. To be humble is to be surrendered to the truth that we are human, mortal, finite, and imperfect, while he toward whom we press is immortal, infinite, perfect, and glorified. To be humble is to be ever aware of the chasm between us and our Creator, between us and him who was sent to save us.

"Be thou humble," the Lord counseled President Thomas B. Marsh and, by extension, each one of us, "and the Lord thy God shall lead thee by the hand, and give thee answer to thy prayers" (D&C 112:10). We are humbled by the truth that we are not and cannot be independent of powers greater than we are. We are humbled by the truth that we must, absolutely must, look to God in order to live. And we are driven to our knees as we comprehend the truth that all our days on this earth—and for aught we know, perhaps even those days that lie ahead beyond the veil of death—we are required to call upon the Father in the name of the Son for everything we have and are and ever hope to become.

We live in a constant state of dependence. And yet as we begin to "grow up unto the Lord" (Helaman 3:21), we sense that such dependence is not a bad thing at all. In fact, it is quite a marvelous thing indeed, for through relying upon Christ completely, wholly (2 Nephi 31:19; Moroni 6:4), we come to draw upon his enabling and sustaining powers, and by this means our God transforms weakness into strength (2 Corinthians 12:9–10; Ether 12:27). "And inasmuch as you have humbled yourselves before me, the blessings of the kingdom are yours" (D&C 61:37). We pray, and God answers. We thereby learn, are reminded, are chastened, are comforted, are challenged, are strengthened, are inspired.

There is a whole host of ways in which our Heavenly Father and our Savior may choose to communicate with us and sustain us. One way is certainly through the workings of our minds, through our thoughts. The Prophet Joseph Smith explained that the spirit of revelation may take the form of "sudden strokes of ideas" flowing into us.[1] Enos, son of Jacob, wrote that the voice of the Lord came into his mind, affirming that his sins had been forgiven (Enos 1:5). On many occasions I have pleaded with the Lord for direction in the preparation of a lesson or a sermon. Often I have been for a time unsure, unclear about the course I should pursue, only to sense, at a certain point in my preparation, that ideas in the form of scriptural passages, prophetic or apostolic statements, and even overall organization have begun to flow into my mind. Similarly, it has been my experience scores of times to be speaking or teaching in a certain avenue, only to have a related idea, experience, or unusual insight make its way onto the stage of my mind. I have never been disappointed when I have responded positively and actively to such promptings, and I have come away from such experiences knowing more surely that God is God, that he knows his children and their individual needs far better than I, and that it is in my best interest as his servant to follow where he leads.

In many cases answers to our prayers come through promptings as we read and ponder on holy scripture. We may well read of Peter's and Paul's doings or sayings and find immediate application to our own lives. We may study where Nephi sought the revelations of heaven, inasmuch as he knew that God was no respecter of persons and would grant to him as He had to Lehi (1 Nephi 10:17–19), and we thereby feel motivated and prompted to do the same. Or, we may be reading along in a section of scripture only to find our minds caught away to serious contemplation on another matter and soon come to realize that this mental detour was planned and orchestrated by the Lord.

"What a glorious blessing!" Elder Robert D. Hales exulted. "For when we want to speak to God, we pray. And when we want Him to speak to us, we search the scriptures; for His words are spoken through His prophets. He will then teach us as we listen to the promptings of the Holy Spirit."[2]

President Boyd K. Packer pointed out: "These delicate, refined spiritual communications are not seen with our eyes nor heard with our ears. And even though it is described as a voice, it is a voice that one feels more than one hears."[3] Revelation, divine communication from God through the Spirit, thus comes to both mind and heart (D&C 8:2–3). In a letter addressed to the Saints in Nauvoo, Joseph Smith wrote: "I now resume the subject of the baptism for the dead, as that subject seems to occupy my mind, and *press itself upon my feelings* the strongest" (D&C 128:1; emphasis added).

A feeling often associated with divine guidance, and yet often overlooked, is the simple feeling of peace. The Savior reminded Oliver Cowdery of the powerful revelation he had previously received while residing in the

Smith home in Palmyra, when he had called upon God to
know of the truthfulness of the claims of the Smith family
regarding young Joseph: "If you desire a further witness,
cast your mind upon the night that you cried unto me in
your heart, that you might know concerning the truth of
these things. Did I not speak peace to your mind concerning the matter? What greater witness can you have than
from God?" (D&C 6:22–23).

"With God, all things are possible," President Thomas
S. Monson reminds us. He explains that "prayer is the
provider of spiritual strength; it is the passport to peace.
Prayer is the means by which we approach our Father
in Heaven, who loves us. Speak to Him in prayer and
then listen for the answer. Miracles are wrought through
prayer."[4]

At the convocation of the College of Education at
Brigham Young University in the summer of 1992, one
student shared with her fellow graduates and others present a touching story about an experience she had had
with a young Native American boy. He had been la-
beled by previous teachers as incorrigible, which was, of
course, a serious problem. She felt impelled to reach out
to him and help. She knew the family situation was difficult and thought that if she visited his home she might
find some clue for how to reach him. The visit stunned
her. She found poverty, neglect, alcoholism, drug abuse—
everything negative and destructive seemed to be present
in that home. Her heart ached for the boy; his situation
made her despondent. As she poured out her heart in

prayer to the Lord, she found herself asking, "Have you forgotten this boy?"

The answer came, quietly and reassuringly: "No. That is why I sent you."

Very often the Almighty answers people's prayers—the prayers of the lonely, the downtrodden, the hungry, the bitter—through other people, through those sensitive souls who open themselves to inspiration and are willing to be inconvenienced.

Chapter 7

WHEN NO CLEAR ANSWER COMES

The Spirit of the Lord is not something that may be programmed, plotted out, manufactured, or elicited; the influence of the Holy Ghost certainly cannot be demanded or coerced. We cannot force spiritual things. Jesus said to Nicodemus: "Marvel not that I said unto thee, Ye must be born again. The wind bloweth where it listeth, and thou hearest the sound thereof, but canst not tell whence it cometh, and whither it goeth: so is every one that is born of the Spirit" (John 3:7–8). The Prophet Joseph Smith likewise taught that "a man may receive the Holy Ghost, and it may descend upon him and not tarry with him" (D&C 130:23). We know that the Spirit will not dwell with those who are unclean and thus unworthy of its companionship (1 Corinthians 3:16–17; 6:19; compare 1 Nephi 10:21; 15:34; Alma 7:21; 3 Nephi 27:19).

In addition, we cannot always tell when we will be filled with the Spirit and when we will not. We may end the day on fire with the power of the Spirit, rejoicing in our blessings, grateful for the closeness we have felt to the Lord. When we arise a few short hours later, it would not be uncommon to feel as though we had lost something, to feel that the distance between us and Deity had increased dramatically. We ask ourselves, "What happened? Did we do something to change what we were feeling only a short time ago?"

President Joseph F. Smith taught that "every elder of the Church who has received the Holy Ghost by the laying on of hands, by one having authority, has power to confer that gift upon another; it does not follow that a man who has received the presentation or gift of the Holy Ghost shall always receive the recognition and witness and presence of the Holy Ghost himself, or he may receive all these, and yet the Holy Ghost not tarry with him, but visit him from time to time." President Smith also observed that "the Holy Spirit, or the Holy Ghost, may be conferred upon men, and he may dwell with them for a while, or he may continue to dwell with them in accordance with their worthiness, and he may depart from them at his will."[1]

Just because we may not always recognize the workings of the Spirit in our lives does not mean that the Spirit is not with us. In looking back over the past forty years of my life, I find that I have had a variety of experiences with the Spirit and with receiving answers to prayer. Many prayers have been answered so directly, so clearly, so unambiguously that there was no doubt as to the course I should follow. On the other hand, many times when I have gone before the Lord in deep sincerity, hungering and thirsting for insight and direction, I have pondered and prayed and pleaded and wrestled and waited upon the Lord. So far as I could tell, I was not guilty of serious sin, and yet no clear answer was forthcoming. President Brigham Young taught us what our course should be in such cases: "If I do not know the will of my Father, and what He requires of me in a certain transaction, if I ask Him to give me wisdom concerning any requirement in life, or in regard to my own course, or that of my friends, my family, my children, or those that I preside over, and get no answer from Him, and then do the very best that my judgment will teach me, He is bound to own and honor that transaction, and He will do so to all intents and purposes."[2]

I believe there is more to President Young's counsel than meets the eye. It is certainly true that we should pray with all our hearts for direction and then make the wisest decisions we can. It is my conviction, however, that even on those occasions when we feel so very alone—when we wonder if God is listening—if we are trusting in our Lord and Savior and relying upon his marvelous merits, the Lord is nonetheless directing our paths, for he has so promised us. No doubt there are seasons of our life when we are called upon to proceed without the clear recognition of the Spirit. Yet that does not mean we are alone. I believe that one day, when we are allowed to review the scenes of mortality from a grander perspective, we will be astounded at how closely the Lord directed our paths, orchestrated the events of our lives, and in general led us by that kindly light we know as the Holy Ghost.

Perhaps it is the case that over the years the Spirit of the Lord works in a quiet but consistent manner to educate our consciences, enhance our perspective, and polish our wisdom and judgment. After all, the Prophet Joseph explained that one of the major assignments of the Holy Ghost was to convey pure intelligence through "expanding the mind, enlightening the understanding, and storing the intellect with present knowledge."[3] It may be that one day we will look back on what we perceived at the time to be a season in which we were required to make decisions on our own, only to discover that the Lord had been, through the honing and refining processes in our souls, leading us along in paths of his choosing. That is, maybe we will learn that our own wisdom and judgment were not really our own.

Sometimes answers to our prayers do not come as quickly as we would like. We try and try again, too often concluding that God must not love us, must not hear us, or must have chosen not to answer. "The answers to our prayers come in the Lord's due time," President Dieter F. Uchtdorf explained. "Sometimes we may become frustrated that the Lord has delayed answering our prayers. In such times we need to understand that He knows what we do not know. He sees what we do not see. Trust in Him. He knows what is best for His child, and being a perfect God, He will answer our prayers perfectly and in the perfect time."[4]

Finally, it is worth noting that we may well have an experience with the Spirit, a genuine and true experience, and yet not know exactly what has taken place. Over the years it has been my privilege to work with Latter-day Saints who were struggling to repent of their sins and become clean before God. It has been one of the joys of Church service to witness the light growing in the countenance, the heart being softened, and the consciousness of right and wrong returning. But never in all my years has a member of the Church said to me, "I have been justified of the Spirit" or "I have entered the rest of God" or "I am redeemed of the Lord" or "I am born of the Spirit." Those who have had their sins remitted and have renewed their covenant with Christ could, in fact, use any of those doctrinal phrases to describe their state or standing, and I would understand what they meant. Generally, they have said such things as "I feel good all over" or "I feel clean and pure" or "I am at peace."

During the period of darkness before his visit to the Americas, Jesus spoke to the Nephites. "I am the light and the life of the world," he said. "I am Alpha and Omega, the beginning and the end. And ye shall offer up unto me no more the shedding of blood; yea, your sacrifices and your burnt offerings shall be done away, for I will accept none of your sacrifices and your burnt offerings. And ye shall offer for a sacrifice unto me a broken heart and a contrite spirit. And whoso cometh unto me with a broken heart and a contrite spirit, him will I baptize with fire and with the Holy Ghost, *even as the Lamanites, because of their faith in me at the time of their conversion, were bap-tized with fire and with the Holy Ghost,* and they knew it not" (3 Nephi 9:18–20; emphasis added; see also Helaman 5). Far more significant than a theological explanation is the value of a religious experience; whether we can give a ten-minute discourse on spiritual rebirth matters but little when compared to the change of heart that such a rebirth brings.

The work of the kingdom—whether at 47 East South Temple Street in Salt Lake City or at our own address—goes forward hour by hour and day by day, even when the path is not clear for the time being. "Salvation cannot come without revelation," Joseph Smith declared. "It is in vain for anyone to minister without it."[5] The Almighty has promised to point the way, and so we trust in his promises and wait upon him "in all patience and faith" (D&C 21:5), though on occasion we cry out, essentially,

> *Lead, kindly Light, amid th' encircling gloom;*
> *Lead thou me on!*
> *The night is dark, and I am far from home;*
> *Lead thou me on!*
> *Keep thou my feet; I do not ask to see*
> *The distant scene—one step enough for me.*[6]

Answers have come. Answers will continue to come, for "we believe that [God] will yet reveal many great and important things pertaining to the kingdom of God" (Articles of Faith 1:9). God does not want us to proceed along the path of life on our own.

Chapter 8

FASTING AND PRAYER

As Jesus and his three chief apostles made their way down the hill after the transcendent and sublime experiences atop the Mount of Transfiguration, he was approached by a distraught man who pleaded for his intervention.

"Lord, have mercy on my son," he cried out, "for he is lunatick, and sore vexed: for ofttimes he falleth into the fire, and oft into the water.

"And I brought him to thy disciples, and they could not cure him.

"Then Jesus answered and said, O faithless and perverse generation, how long shall I be with you? how long shall I suffer you? bring him hither to me.

"And Jesus rebuked the devil; and he departed out of him: and the child was cured from that very hour.

"Then came the disciples to Jesus apart, and said, Why could not we cast him out?

"And Jesus said unto them, Because of your unbelief

[little faith]: for verily I say unto you, If ye have faith as a grain of mustard seed, ye shall say unto this mountain, Remove hence to yonder place; and it shall remove; and nothing shall be impossible unto you.

"Howbeit *this kind goeth not out but by prayer and fasting*" (Matthew 17:15–21; emphasis added).

A curious episode in the ministry of the Master, is it not? What more does one need than the priesthood of Almighty God? What greater power could one have than the holy apostleship? And yet the apostles failed to deliver a person from the burden of demonic possession. The reason? Their faith was insufficient. Some circumstances clearly require an added effort, an extended measure of spirituality, that will translate into the faith necessary to work a mighty miracle. In this case, Jesus suggested that the apostles might well have engaged in prayer and fasting to better prepare themselves to pull down the powers of heaven.

Through the prophet Isaiah some seven centuries before, Jehovah had revealed his mind and will concerning the vital place of fasting: "Is not this the fast that I have chosen? to loose the bands of wickedness, to undo the heavy burdens, and to let the oppressed go free, and that ye break every yoke?" (Isaiah 58:6).

We fast to overcome wickedness, to dismiss evil from our lives, to obtain a remission of sins. We fast and pray to alleviate heavy burdens—the heaviest of which is sin—to set people free from the power of the destroyer, to break the bands of transgression and shift from the galling yoke of waywardness to the light and easy yoke of Jesus (Matthew 11:29–30). And what is it about fasting that can accomplish such wonders? What does fasting do that prayer alone cannot do?

Nothing is more central to the lives of mortal beings than food. We eat to live and, in some cases, we live to eat. Fasting allows us to place the emphasis where it ought to be, to prepare our food "with singleness of heart" (D&C 59:13; compare Acts 2:46), to gain control of our appetites and subject our flesh to our spirit. During a fast, the physical body craves, but the spirit chooses to curtail. While the body demands to be fed, the spirit within us, the will, elects to go without. That simple act of self-mastery aids us immeasurably in drawing closer to God. As President David O. McKay taught, "Spirituality is the consciousness of victory over self, and of communion with the Infinite."[1]

It is not just that through fasting we gain victory over self; it is also that *we know* we have gained that victory: we are victors, and we are conscious of it. That awareness, that consciousness of victory over self, that sacrifice of a lesser good for a greater, plants within us the quiet and powerful confidence that is the essence of faith. The Prophet Joseph Smith taught that we come to saving faith because we possess an actual knowledge that our course in life is pleasing to God.[2]

Further, when we add to our fast a fast offering, a free-will donation of our resources for the care of the poor, we add another dimension to this marvelous principle and practice. Fasting focuses us upon hunger, upon need, and, if we will so direct our thoughts and desires, upon those who go hungry every day, those who know the bitter pangs of poverty and want twenty-four hours a day, seven days a week. Fasting thus directs us toward our own prosperity and the awful alienation of those who frequently go without. Consequently, as we fast and pray not only for our own special blessing but also for the poor and the needy, and as we help to answer that prayer through being generous in our offerings, we involve ourselves in the great work of our Master. King Benjamin explained that as we acknowledge our own bankruptcy without our Lord, as we surrender our nothingness to his everything, and as we give of our physical and emotional surplus to help the needy, we place ourselves in a frame of mind and heart to retain a remission of our sins from day to day (Mosiah 4:11–12, 26).

Fasting feeds faith. Fasting brings joy. Fasting, linked with prayer, creates an attitude of gratitude. Fasting and prayer are, in fact, the same as rejoicing and prayer (D&C 59:13–15). When we fast and pray, we hunger and thirst after righteousness. Fasting and prayer work miracles, for they demonstrate to the Almighty that we are serious in seeking this particular blessing, serious enough to deny ourselves of that which pleases the eye and gladdens the heart, that which strengthens the body and enlivens the soul (D&C 59:18–19). Fasting is a sublime form of spiritual discipline, and the glorious outcome is dedicated and dynamic Christian discipleship.

Chapter 9

WHEN WE DON'T
FEEL LIKE PRAYING

One Saturday morning our family slept in and consequently had to rush about like wild people to get ready to leave for my wife's family reunion in the Salt Lake City area, some forty miles north of where we lived. One son yelled at another one for taking his socks, and one daughter pouted that she couldn't find anything to wear, declaring that she simply wasn't going. My wife, Shauna, dressed herself and some of the younger ones and packed her materials for the activity she was to conduct at the reunion. It was pandemonium. Chaos. There was little beauty all around, since there was very little love felt at home that morning. To complicate matters, it was necessary for us to take two cars, because neither had sufficient seating for all of us. And even then we knew we would be squeezed together like sardines for an hour there and an hour back. O happy day!

In the midst of all the rushing about, attempting to assign the right personalities to the right car, Shauna suggested that we ought to have prayer before we left. Some moaned, some groaned, and some just went silent. But I agreed with the suggestion and felt a bit guilty that it hadn't come from me. So I bowed my head, asked the bunch to bow theirs, and I mumbled a prayer, sincere to be sure but nonetheless rushed. Then we set off.

We had been on the road only a short time when I noticed that about three hundred yards ahead a truck seemed to be getting awfully close to the car Shauna was driving. Suddenly the truck's front bumper clipped Shauna's rear bumper, and her car went spinning across the highway, doing 360s. Those of us in the car I was driving panicked and froze, but I managed to pull over to the shoulder. We watched with terror as our family members spun into harm's way.

Although the freeway had been packed with traffic, for some blessed reason Shauna was soon able to move from the freeway onto the right shoulder without being struck by an oncoming vehicle. There was silence in my car for about twenty seconds, and then some began to cry. We drove quickly up the shoulder until we were immediately behind our loved ones. The autos emptied, and in shock we tearfully hugged and cried together. After ten or fifteen minutes of collecting ourselves and then offering a prayer of thanksgiving, we climbed back into our respective cars and resumed our journey.

As you might suppose, I did some pretty heavy contemplation on the way to the reunion. I continued to offer thanks to God, thanks for preserving the lives of my loved ones, and thanks, yes, for listening and responding affirmatively to our initial prayer. We almost didn't have time for it. No, that is not correct: we almost didn't *make* time for it. My faith is simple enough to believe that our prayer, hurried and hectic as it was, made a difference.

I am always a bit hesitant to relate this story, given that occasionally a loved one's prayer for safety is followed by an accident. I do not want to be insensitive to those painful situations in which the answer to a petition seems to have been no; I know that happens. But I also believe, as James teaches, that the "effectual fervent prayer of a righteous man" or woman does avail much (James 5:16).

Sometimes we simply don't feel like praying. Maybe it's the end of a long and busy and tiresome day, and we're exhausted. Maybe the mood in the home or the Church meeting was anything but encouraging. Maybe we feel as though our prayers have recently been bouncing off the ceiling, that our words have been empty, and that God is not listening.

President Lorenzo Snow felt that way: "Some two or three weeks after I was baptized, one day while engaged in my studies, I began to reflect upon the fact that I had not obtained a *knowledge* of the truth of the work—that I had not realized the fulfilment of the promise 'he that doeth my will shall know of the doctrine,' and I began to feel very uneasy. I laid aside my books, left the house, and wandered around through the fields under the oppressive influence of a gloomy, disconsolate spirit, while an indescribable cloud of darkness seemed to envelop me.

"I had been accustomed, at the close of the day, to retire for secret prayer, to a grove a short distance from my lodgings, but at this time I felt no inclination to do so. The spirit of prayer had departed and the heavens seemed like brass over my head. At length, realizing that the usual time had come for secret prayer, I concluded I would not forego my evening service, and, as a matter of formality, knelt as I was in the habit of doing, and in my accustomed retired place, but not feeling as I was wont to feel.

"I had no sooner opened my lips in an effort to pray, than I heard a sound, just above my head, like the rustling of silken robes, and immediately the Spirit of God descended upon me, completely enveloping my whole person, filling me, from the crown of my head to the soles of my feet, and O, the joy and happiness I felt! No language can describe the almost instantaneous transition from a dense cloud of mental and spiritual darkness into a refulgence of light and knowledge, as it was at that time imparted to my understanding. I then received a perfect knowledge that God lives, that Jesus Christ is the Son of God, and of the restoration of the holy Priesthood, and the fulness of the Gospel.

"It was a complete baptism—a tangible immersion in the heavenly principle or element, the Holy Ghost; and even more real and physical in its effects upon every part of my system than the immersion by water; dispelling forever, so long as reason and memory last, all possibility of doubt or fear in relation to the fact handed down to us historically, that the 'Babe of Bethlehem' is truly the Son of God; also the fact that He is now being revealed to the children of men, and communicating knowledge, the same as in the Apostolic times. I was perfectly satisfied, as well I might be, for my expectations were more than realized, I think I may safely say in an infinite degree.

"I cannot tell how long I remained in the full flow of the blissful enjoyment and divine enlightenment, but it was several minutes before the celestial element which filled and surrounded me began gradually to withdraw. On arising from my kneeling posture, with my heart swelling with gratitude to God, beyond the power of expression, I felt—I *knew* that He had conferred on me what only an omnipotent being can confer—that which is of greater value than all the wealth and honors worlds can bestow.

"That night, as I retired to rest, the same wonderful manifestations were repeated, and continued to be for several successive nights. The sweet remembrance of those glorious experiences, from that time to the present, bring them fresh before me, imparting an inspiring influence which pervades my whole being, and I trust will to the close of my earthly existence."[1]

President Snow didn't really feel like praying, but he prayed anyway. In his heart of hearts he knew it was the right thing to do. It is always better to do the right thing for the wrong reason than it is to do the wrong thing. Very often when we persist, even when our heart and mind aren't into the prayer, good and great things come to pass. The Father of Light honors our prayers, and he always hears them.

"It matters not whether you or I feel like praying," President Brigham Young declared, "when the time comes to pray, *pray*. If we do not feel like it, we should pray till we *do*. . . . You will find that those who wait till the Spirit bids them pray will never pray much on this earth."[2]

On another occasion he observed: "Our judgment teaches us that it is our duty to pray, whether we are particularly in the spirit of praying or not. My doctrine is, it is [our] duty to pray; and when the time for prayer comes, John should say, 'This is the place and this is the time to pray: knees bend down upon that floor, and do so at once.' . . . If I could not master my mouth, I would my knees, and make them bend until my mouth would speak."[3] Prayer is a significant spiritual discipline, a sublime labor we perform—even when we do not feel like doing so—because we know that the fruits are sweet and the results will minister to our edification. I rather suspect that there was a meaningful decrease in spiritual inertia in the heart of Lorenzo Snow the next time he felt some hesitation to pray.

And so it is with us: we pray because we should; we pray because we ought to; we pray because we must. And in many cases we pray because it is the only thing we know to do. In the long run God is glorified, and we are blessed.

Chapter 10

OUR WORDS MATTER

M ore than once through the years I have been told, "Be careful what you pray. You just may get what you ask for." At first that sounded pretty good to me: What's the problem with getting everything you ask for, anyway?

I have now lived long enough to appreciate the counsel, and I can bear a solid witness that sometimes we are too shallow in our perspectives, too short-sighted in our requests. The apostle Paul stated a mighty truth when he suggested that sometimes we do not know what to pray for as we ought, and consequently we need the mediation of the Holy Spirit to purify us and give direction to our prayers (Romans 8:26–27). Indeed, we will spend a lifetime struggling in the Spirit to get our hearts right, our desires educated, our consciences refined.

Many years ago I heard Elder Dallin H. Oaks recount to students at Brigham Young University how his widowed mother had pleaded repeatedly with her children to "pray about your feelings."¹ I was so touched by that simple direction that I think I have not offered many prayers since then in which I have not asked God to help me to feel what I ought to feel and think what I ought to think. I have come to realize that such a request of our Heavenly Father is really a request to be born again, renewed in mind and heart, "changed from [our] carnal and fallen state, to a state of righteousness, being redeemed of God, becoming his sons and daughters" (Mosiah 27:25). It is more than a cosmetic alteration, far more than behavior modification. It is an inner renovation, a metamorphosis from the inside out. The father of King Lamoni in the Book of Mormon cried out to Aaron: "What shall I do that I may have this eternal life of which thou hast spoken? Yea, what shall I do that I may be born of God, having this wicked spirit rooted out of my breast, and receive his Spirit, that I may be filled with joy, that I may not be cast off at the last day?" (Alma 22:15). Each of us, like the old king, must be willing to give up all that we possess, even our individual kingdoms. Further, we must be willing to give away all our sins in order to truly know the God whose face we seek (Alma 22:15–18; D&C 101:38).

During the late 1980s I was asked to travel to another part of the country to assist the Latter-day Saints in that area to face and respond properly to anti-Mormonism. A temple had recently been dedicated there, and, as is so often the case, enemies of the Church came out of the woodwork. I spoke in one town on Thursday night, and all went well. On Friday night I delivered the same message to members of the Church in a nearby city. On Saturday morning I slept in a bit, arose, went for a walk, and returned to the motel. I read and worked on a few projects for several hours that day. An early dinner was followed by a glance at the television to check on sports scores. After getting dressed for the presentation I was to give that evening, I knelt beside the bed and prayed. There was nothing particularly unusual about this occasion; I thanked the Lord for the good experiences of the two preceding nights and asked for his help one more time. Then I heard myself say, "Father, I want to do what's right and what thou wouldst have done. Tell me what to say, and I will say it. Tell me what not to say, and I won't say it." It was a rather odd request, I thought at the time, but I didn't make much of it.

A local member of the Church picked me up ten or fifteen minutes later, and we drove to the stake center. While sitting on the stand and as the time when I was to deliver my message drew closer, a deep discomfort began to fill my soul. As I considered my speech on how to deal with opposition, I felt sick. During the musical number that preceded my talk, I leaned over to the stake president and said, "President, I have a problem."

"What's the matter?" he asked. "You don't look so good."

I told him I felt quite uncomfortable speaking on the subject of opposition. Yet this particular presentation had been advertised for several months, and I didn't want to disappoint the four hundred or five hundred Saints at the meeting.

He smiled and said gently, "Then, Brother Millet, you stand up and tell the people what the Lord wants you to say."

I felt a few seconds' comfort, for part one of my problem was solved. I knew clearly what was *not* to be discussed, but part two was to find out what topic *was* to be addressed. At that moment the musical number ended.

A speaker can take up only so much time telling the congregation how lovely it is to be there, how wonderful the area is, how delightful it is to be a part of the Church Educational System, etc., etc. I prayed with all my heart to know what to do and what to say. There was no private agenda on my part, no favorite subject I was longing to discuss. After a few minutes of feeling my way through the darkness, the light came on. It became clear to me that I was, for some reason, to speak on what modern prophets and the scriptures of the Restoration have taught us concerning life after death. I glanced at my briefcase near my feet. It was filled with information about opposition, but all that I had to assist me in speaking on this new topic were my scriptures and a copy of *Teachings of the Prophet Joseph Smith*. And, of course, I had access to the Spirit of the Lord.

This was one of those occasions that come rarely in a lifetime. For well over an hour I spoke on this subject with no notes, nothing but the earnest desire of my heart to do this subject justice. I learned a great deal that night from what I had to say, and I felt the congregation did as well.[2] My tongue was loosed, and I enjoyed a fluency of speech I had never before experienced. The words and writings and teachings of Church leaders flooded into my mind, and I spoke them.

When I sat down, I looked over at the stake president. He was very sober, and I feared I had disappointed him or been inappropriate in some way. After the closing prayer and as members of the congregation began to make their way toward us to shake hands, the stake president said that he would like to speak briefly with me later.

When everyone else had left, the stake president and I sat together. He asked, "Do you know why you chose to speak on life after death?" I shook my head. He said, "Brother Millet, one of the members of our stake died a few days ago. It was a tragic death, one that raised many questions about why the Lord would allow such things to happen. A funeral was held for the young man in this chapel late this afternoon. Even after the services, many people had concerns about life here and life hereafter. The Lord blessed you tonight, Brother Millet. You addressed most of those questions in your talk. Thank you."

After the president and I had finished our chat, a few stake members invited us to join them for a late snack. I thanked them for their offer but indicated that I was very tired and needed to get some rest. Actually, though, what I wanted to do most right then was to return to the motel, kneel beside my bed once again, and thank a gracious Lord for allowing me to be a part of something significant.

I think often of that unusual experience, and it reminds me that God Almighty is in charge—that this is his work, and it must be done in his own way and according to his will. I am weak, ever so weak, when it comes to speaking the words of truth, but I know, as Ammon humbly affirmed, that "in [God's] strength I can do all things" (Alma 26:12; compare Philippians 4:13). Our task is to repent and improve and read and study and prepare and pray and plead for divine assistance. And when the time is right, God will work through us to bless his children. What the Lord said in regard to the early missionaries in this dispensation is to some degree true of each of us who seeks to be led and empowered by his Spirit: "And ye shall *go forth in the power of my Spirit, preaching my gospel,* two by two, in my name, lifting up your voices as with the sound of a trump, *declaring my word like unto angels of God*" (D&C 42:6; emphasis added).

Another lesson to be learned from this experience is simply this: Our words matter. What we say when we lift our voices heavenward is important. If we are careful, if we are spiritually attentive, if we are unselfish and patient, then the Lord may send his Spirit to prompt the very words we speak, as I believe he did with me that Saturday afternoon in the motel. And the beauty of that kind of prayer is that the Lord always answers it (D&C 46:30).

Sanctification is a lifetime process. It is the means by which we, as partakers of the blessings of the sacred Atonement, are purified and come to love the things that may have been distasteful to us in our spiritual immaturity. By the purging and enabling power of the Spirit, God creates a clean heart and renews a right spirit within us (Psalm 51:10). We grow gradually into the spirit of revelation, begin to feel passionate about becoming a holy person, and thereby come to desire the things God desires. We can become like Nephi, son of Helaman, to whom the Lord God spoke the following sublime words: "Blessed art thou, Nephi, for those things which thou hast done; for I have beheld how thou hast with unwearying-ness declared the word. . . . And now, because thou hast done this . . . , behold, I will bless thee forever; and I will make thee mighty in word and in deed, in faith and in works; yea, even that all things shall be done unto thee according to thy word, for thou shalt not ask that which is contrary to my will" (Helaman 10:4–5).

What trust! What honor! And what a blessing that we all seek. And yes, it is obtainable; it is within reach.

Chapter 11

HELP FROM THOSE ON THE OTHER SIDE

Aↄswers to prayer usually come in quiet ways to mortals through the mediation of the Holy Spirit and through the intervention of other mortals. There are times, however, when God chooses to do the unusual— to give visions or dreams, to send angels from the courts of glory, in short, to minister to our needs in truly spectacular ways. Nephi explained that on certain occasions God "hath heard my cry by day, and he hath given me knowledge by visions in the nighttime. And by day have I waxed bold in mighty prayer before him; yea, my voice have I sent up on high; and angels came down and ministered unto me" (2 Nephi 4:23–24).

An intensely personal experience my family and I had some years ago demonstrates just how thin the veil is sometimes. One of our children had chosen to separate himself not only from Church activity but also from family association. He became heavily involved with addictive drugs and buried himself in a hellish world that held out little hope for a return to normal living. Shauna and I prayed and wrestled and yearned for his recovery and return, but we heard nothing from him, and we were left to wonder whether our son was dead, imprisoned, or lost. No word had come in many months, and the burden of pain and awful anticipation of a notification of incarceration or drug overdose grew heavier each day. One night as Shauna and I knelt in prayer, broken and torn emotionally and physically weak from worry, we wept through our prayers and pleaded long and hard, once again, for the Good Shepherd to lead his wandering sheep home. We went to bed and slept from sorrow.

Sometime during that night I found myself dreaming. My father, who had passed away several years before, came to me in the dream, embraced me, and then looked me in the eye. He said quite forcefully, "Son, I want you to pull yourself together. I am going to help you with those children of yours. Be patient."

I awoke and immediately sat up in bed. My sudden movement wakened Shauna. "What's wrong? What happened?" she asked.

I explained that I had seen Dad in a dream and he had told me he would help with our wanderer. Shauna and I both wept as deep feelings of gratitude and reassurance flowed into our souls.

Days later the phone rang in the middle of the night. Our son said, "I just can't live like this any more. Can I come home?"

We were so thrilled to hear from him, so grateful to

know that he was still alive, that we felt no need to set the terms or specify under what conditions he could return. We simply welcomed him home with tender affection.

One evening a few weeks later, he and I were sitting on the sofa in the living room. He turned to me and said hesitantly, "Dad, I need to share something with you."

I nodded and encouraged him to proceed.

He continued, "I know this sounds strange, but one night some time back, I was on the verge of doing something that would definitely have cost me my life when I heard Grandpa Millet's voice say, 'Don't do that! You have been taught better. Now get up and go home.' Dad, is that too weird to be true?"

With some emotion I answered that it was not and added, "Now I have a story to tell you." I then told him of my dream.

We felt the Spirit of the Lord resting upon us and sensed that the entire experience was true and from God. We embraced.

My father was a wonderful man who loved his children and his grandchildren. He did all he could to assist us while he was alive. Without question, however, his greatest influence on my family—which, of course, is his family, too—has come since he passed through the veil of death and has been allowed to minister on occasion to loved ones.

President Joseph F. Smith, in a general conference

address in April of 1916, made the following impressive and instructive remarks:

"Sometimes the Lord expands our vision from this point of view and this side of the veil, so that we feel and seem to realize that we can look beyond the thin veil which separates us from that other sphere. If we can see, by the enlightening influence of the Spirit of God and through the words that have been spoken by the holy prophets of God, beyond the veil that separates us from the spirit world, surely those who have passed beyond, can see more clearly through the veil back here to us than it is possible for us to see to them from our sphere of action. I believe we move and have our being in the presence of heavenly messengers and of heavenly beings. We are not separate from them.

"We begin to realize, more and more fully, as we become acquainted with the principles of the gospel, as they have been revealed anew in this dispensation, that we are closely related to our kindred, to our ancestors, to our friends and associates and co-laborers who have preceded us into the spirit world. We can not forget them; we do not cease to love them; we always hold them in our hearts, in memory. . . .

"How much more certain it is and reasonable and consistent to believe that those who have been faithful, who have gone beyond and are still engaged in the work for the salvation of the souls of men, . . . can see us better than we can see them; that they know us better than we know them. They have advanced; we are advancing; we are growing as they have grown; we are reaching the goal that they have attained unto; and therefore, I claim that we live in their presence, they see us, they are solicitous for our welfare, they love us now more than ever. For now they see the dangers that beset us; they can comprehend, better than ever before, the weaknesses that are liable to mislead us into dark and forbidden paths. They see the temptations and the evils that beset us in life and the proneness of mortal beings to yield to temptation and to wrong doing; hence their solicitude for us, and their love for us, and their desire for our well being, must be greater than that which we feel for ourselves."[1]

President George Albert Smith likewise emphasized that "those who are on the other side [of the veil] are . . . anxious about us. They are praying for us and for our success. They are pleading, in their own way, for their descendants, for their posterity who live upon the earth."[2]

What could possibly be more important to me when I die than whether my children and grandchildren come unto Christ and walk in his covenants blamelessly? "I have no greater joy," John wrote as a very old man, "than to hear that my children walk in truth" (3 John 1:4). Elder Russell M. Nelson explained, "salvation is an individual matter; exaltation is a family matter."[3] We cannot be perfect, or fully happy, for that matter, without being joined with our family members in the exalted state, a welding link having been established between the parents and the children (Hebrews 11:40; D&C 128:15, 18). Consequently, we pray with all our hearts here for our family to be united in the gospel covenant. Those prayers will continue in the postmortal world of spirits, with at least the same intensity, when we finish our work on this earth. The work of the Lord goes forward on both sides of the veil.

Chapter 12

PETITIONS GOD DELIGHTS TO HONOR

Let us consider what things the Lord is eager to hear mentioned in prayer, matters that he delights to hear of, answers he desires to give. Allow me to be a bit personal.

I began praying more than forty years ago that God would grant me a deeper understanding of the restored gospel. I have known of the truthfulness of the prophetic call of Joseph Smith all my life, and I have been unaffected by the railing accusations of the critics of the Church. But it has never been enough for me just to know this work is true. I have yearned, with great zeal and energy, to be enlightened and better informed of the tenets of the faith, the doctrines of salvation, so that I could teach and expound its truths more effectively. I have always known it is true, but I have wanted more, much more—to know *why* it is true. I have pleaded with the Lord long and hard to grant unto me, in the words of Peter, first, the ability to provide an answer to anyone who asks me about my faith, and second, to provide a reason for the hope within me (1 Peter 3:15). I have not asked to know more than I should know or to know it all right now. Rather, I have tried to be patient; I have asked the Lord to grant unto me, line upon line and precept upon precept, insights into the plan of salvation, the Fall, the Atonement, the mercy and grace of God, the love of God, charity, the gifts and fruit of the Spirit, the priesthood, and a host of other topics. I have learned by personal experience that our beloved Father in Heaven is kind, willing to share, and eager that we all mature in our gospel understandings.

I began working with men and women of other faiths almost fifteen years ago. I sensed that it was important for me not only to know what I believe but also to understand more completely what they believe. Consequently, I began a major reading program that continues to this day, studying, in addition to the standard works, general conference addresses and Latter-day Saint history and doctrine. Books, articles, conferences, and special lectures have aided me in my quest to know where my brothers and sisters of other faiths are on the religious continuum.

After a while it became clear to me that reading and study, though vital, were insufficient. I also needed to know what they felt, what they valued, what they treasured. I found myself one morning praying as follows: "Heavenly Father, please help me to see my friends of other faiths, to some extent at least, as thou dost see them. Help me to love them as they are loved by thee." I have learned from personal experience that such a prayer is as a sweet savor to the Lord God, and he who is the embodiment of light and life and love and tender mercy is eager to bestow his own love upon us, to empower us to give and serve and care for those all about us, in ways that are far more profound than we could have imagined. I have felt no hesitation on the part of God to grant such a request.

Very early in our marriage, Shauna and I began praying that we might receive heaven's assistance in meeting our financial obligations, wisdom in managing our resources, and help in paying our bills so that eventually we could become debt free. There were, to be sure, many tight places through which we passed, numerous occasions when our faith was tested. And yet in those difficult times we often found our hearts turning to the scriptural promises, and we would pray: "Father in Heaven, we have paid our tithes and offerings, as thou hast commanded. We now call upon thee to open the windows of heaven and pour out a blessing upon us that would enable us to meet our obligations. Our trust is in thee."

As time passed and as we matured in our assessment of what was a need and what was a want, as we sought to follow the counsel of Church leaders to put our house in order and become independent, and as we looked for and recognized opportunities to live within our means so as to become debt free, the Lord was gracious to us. We prospered well beyond what we felt we deserved. God is good, and he is more than willing to open doors and to provide escape from bondage.

How do you think the Lord would feel if we importuned for blessings in such areas as food storage, spiritual gifts, missionary opportunities, chances to lift and serve others, purification of our hearts, opportunities for improved employment, deepened faith, a strengthened and educated conscience, courage to stand up and speak out on moral issues, physical and emotional strength to serve more faithfully in the kingdom, and so forth? We can rest assured that whatever we pray for in the name of Christ— that is good and right—will be given to us in the Lord's due time (3 Nephi 18:20; Moroni 7:26).

"I, the Lord, am merciful and gracious unto those who fear me, and delight to honor those who serve me in righteousness and in truth unto the end. Great shall be their reward and eternal shall be their glory" (D&C 76:5–6). When the desire is good, when the need is great, when the request is proper, we need but to ask.

Chapter 13

SURRENDER IN PRAYER

"God is not only our orchestrator, but our composer," wrote one Christian observer.

"Christ Jesus is the author *and finisher* of our lives. (See Hebrews 12:2.)

"As long [as] we insist on writing our own stories, he cannot write his living will onto our hearts.

"As long as we insist on forging our own paths, he cannot lead us into his paths of righteousness.

"As long as we insist on governing our own lives, he cannot be our sovereign King and Lord.

"As long as we insist on living life according to our own desires, he cannot impart his desires or guide us into his wholeness, fruitfulness, and blessings.

"As long as we feel that we are in control of our fate, we cannot experience fully the destiny he has for us.

"We are *his* workmanship. When we act otherwise, we are breaching our trust relationship with God and are refusing to submit our lives fully to him."[1]

President Boyd K. Packer taught a profound lesson many years ago:

"I knew what agency was and knew how important it was to be individual and to be independent, to be free. I somehow knew there was one thing the Lord would never take from me, and that was my free agency. I would not surrender my agency to any being but to Him! I determined that I would *give* Him the one thing that He would never take—my agency. I decided, by myself, that from that time on I would do things His way.

"That was a great trial for me, for I thought I was giving away the most precious thing I possessed. I was not wise enough in my youth to know that because I exercised my agency and decided myself, I was not *losing* it. It was *strengthened!*"[2]

In a leadership meeting some years later, President Packer spoke very soberly of that time in his life when he had determined to surrender his agency to God. He recommended to the priesthood leaders that we consider doing the same but added, with unaccustomed sternness, that such a surrender is serious and not to be offered lightly.

And indeed it is. We really should not offer something if we have no intention of letting it go. We really should not indicate to the Almighty that we intend to give him something when in fact we are prepared to give him only a portion. There's a rather frightening story in Acts 5 about a man and his wife who ostensibly consecrated their all to the Lord through his apostles, but in reality they kept back a portion of their goods, in case their stewardship or inheritance was not sufficient for their desires. Both Ananias and his wife, Sapphira, died suddenly. "And great fear came upon all the church, and upon as many as heard these things" (Acts 5:11).

To be sure, the Lord seldom strikes people down immediately because of their duplicity, but this story demonstrates powerfully that the Master expects us to be honest about our offering. In fact, what can we offer to God? Our savings accounts? Our properties? Our investments? No, for he already owns all of this world's goods: "The earth is the Lord's, and the fulness thereof; the world, and they that dwell therein" (Psalm 24:1).

Elder Neal A. Maxwell pointed out: "The submission of one's will is really the only uniquely personal thing we have to place on God's altar. The many other things . . . He has already given or loaned to us. However, when you and I finally submit ourselves, by letting our individual wills be swallowed up in God's will, then we are really giving something to Him! It is the only possession which is truly ours to give!

"Consecration thus constitutes the only unconditional surrender which is also a total victory!"[3]

Praying "thy will be done" may entail submitting to difficult or challenging circumstances ahead. C. S. Lewis provided a slightly different approach to the scripture. "'Thy will *be done.*' But a great deal of it is to be done by God's creatures; including me. The petition, then, is not merely that I may patiently suffer God's will but also that

I may vigorously do it. I must be an agent as well as a patient. I am asking that I may be enabled to do it. . . .

"Taken this way, I find the words have a more regular daily application. For there isn't always—or we don't always have reason to suspect that there is—some great affliction looming in the near future, but there are always duties to be done; usually, for me, neglected duties to be caught up with. 'Thy will be done—by me—now' brings one back to brass tacks." Further, Lewis explained, "Thy will be done" may also imply a readiness on our part to receive and experience new and unanticipated blessings. "I know it sounds fantastic; but think it over. It seems to me that we often, almost sulkily, reject the good that God offers us because, at that moment, we expected some other good."[4]

"Thy will be done" thus represents our petition that the Almighty work his wonders through us, that he open our hearts to new ideas, new avenues of understanding, new paths and new doors of opportunity when it is best for us to move in another direction.

Each of us knows deep down that eventually we must surrender to the Lord and open ourselves to his will for us. But not today. Not that way. Surely, we suppose, there will come a time when we will be more prepared to make the sacrifice of self and lay it all on God's altar. But not now. The cold, hard fact is that if we wait until some special, red-letter day to offer our all to the Almighty, the day may never come.

Is there a better day than today? Will there be a better time to repent, a more fitting occasion for improvement or refinement or commitment? Or will we make today a moment that matters, an instant in eternity toward which we will look back with gratitude and thanksgiving for a decision that counted? Truly, as Amulek declared, "now is the time and the day of [our] salvation; and therefore, if [we] will repent and harden not [our] hearts, immediately shall the great plan of redemption be brought about unto [us]" (Alma 34:31; compare 2 Corinthians 6:2).

In the first estate, the premortal world, the great Jehovah declared, "Father, thy will be done, and the glory be thine forever" (Moses 4:2). In Gethsemane, as the hours of atonement began, he said in prayer, "Not my will, but thine, be done" (Luke 22:42; compare Matthew 26:39, Mark 14:36). As he breathed his last breath on the cross of Calvary, Jesus said, as the capstone to his incomparable life, "Father, it is finished, thy will is done." He then "yielded up the ghost" (JST, Matthew 27:54). That sacred submission, combined with his divine inheritance from the Eternal Father, is what made him who he is. That sublime relinquishment of will enabled him to do what no other mortal could do.

There is a lasting lesson here for us. Spiritual growth takes place as we become more and more willing to submit, more and more anxious to learn and carry out the will of him who knows best what to do with us. Through divine grace and assistance (D&C 109:44), we are enabled to see things as they really are, to realize what really matters, and to consecrate our whole souls toward the realization of God's great work and glory.

Chapter 14

PRAYER IN SPIRIT

Perfect prayer is offered to God the Eternal Father, in the name of his Only Begotten Son, by the power of the Holy Ghost. Most of us are well aware that God the Father is the ultimate object of our worship and that our prayers should be directed to him. And we know that we are to pray to Father in the name of the Son. But perhaps we are not quite so familiar with the idea that our prayers, in order to meet the divine standard, should be prompted, guided, and empowered by the Holy Spirit. In other words, as with all forms of divine communication, including sermons, gospel lessons, and so forth, prayers should be carried out under the direction of the third member of the Godhead.

Another way of putting this is to observe that prayer is not, and should not be, merely a product of our own thoughts and feelings. Prayer is intended to engender communion with Deity. Communion certainly entails more than a monologue. It should in fact be a dialog, a true conversation with speaking, listening, digesting, learning. Most of us know how uncomfortable we are with someone who does not allow real conversation, who may ask questions but never allows us to answer. We no doubt have had encounters with a person who delights in finishing our sentences or otherwise providing answers to his or her own questions. At best it is frustrating. At worst it is maddening and extremely impolite. I don't think it's an ego thing alone to desire to speak, to want to be heard. That's what humans do.

From that perspective, then, have you ever pondered upon how our Heavenly Father must feel about a conversation in which you or I do all the talking and even ask critical and important questions but never allow time or silence for his response? Despite our Father's patience, magnanimity, and all-loving nature, it must at least be disappointing to him. "Be still, and know that I am God" (Psalm 46:10; D&C 101:16) is pretty important counsel to us. Maybe it means that after we have finished speaking to God, we should spend a little time listening, possibly remaining on our knees but perhaps sitting quietly and reverently, anticipating that our Father may have something to contribute to our chat. Will we hear a voice? Perhaps, but perhaps not; instead, we may have an inner awareness, a spirit of peace, acceptance, love. We may find our minds turning toward matters that we had not intended to contemplate. We may be sanctified by the solemnity and sublimity of silence.

There is likewise another practice that is spiritually

healthy and profitable to us: seeking to be guided by the Spirit to know what to pray. "He that asketh in the Spirit asketh according to the will of God; wherefore it is done even as he asketh" (D&C 46:30). "And if ye are purified and cleansed from all sin, ye shall ask whatsoever you will in the name of Jesus and it shall be done. But know this, it shall be given you what you shall ask" (D&C 50:29–30). Furthermore, "Let my servants, Joseph Smith, Jun., and Sidney Rigdon, seek them a home, as they are *taught through prayer by the Spirit*" (D&C 63:65; emphasis added). Each of these passages suggests an avenue of divine instruction that can come though prayer. The Lord may choose, through his Spirit, to teach us what we should pray for and actually provide the words for our supplication or petition.

But why would we need God to give us the very words to use in addressing him? Simply stated, "the Spirit also helpeth our infirmities: for we know not what we should pray for as we ought: but the Spirit itself maketh intercession for us with groanings which cannot be uttered" (Romans 8:26), or more correctly, "with striving which cannot be expressed."[1] Paul continued, "And he that searcheth the hearts knoweth what is the mind of the Spirit, because he maketh intercession for the saints according to the will of God" (Romans 8:27). In other words, often we pray for our wants, when in truth it would be wise to pray for our needs. But we generally are unable to discern what is most critical in our lives, what thoughts and feelings and yearnings lie deep within our soul and are not readily accessible to the conscious mind.

We need help. We need mediation. And that is where the Comforter, the Revelator, comes in. The Holy Ghost can, if we are open and teachable and patient, make known to us the things of greatest import, the things upon which God would have us ponder and reflect and pray over. If we will be still, if we will be quiet, if we will be attentive, if we will be sensitive during and after our prayer, we may find our words reaching beyond our thoughts, just as occurred in the New World during the visit of the risen Lord to the Nephites: "And it came to pass that when Jesus had thus prayed unto the Father, he came unto his disciples, and behold, they did still continue, without ceasing, to pray unto him; and they did not multiply many words, for it was given unto them what they should pray, and they were filled with desire" (3 Nephi 19:24).[2]

What a joy to have the Lord inspire us in how we should pray and what words we should speak! Prayer thereby becomes not only petitionary but marvelously instructive, for we often learn something from what we find ourselves saying. Can we see that in this way prayer becomes a major avenue of revelation? Can we see how prayer can open us to the mind of God? Can we fathom the abiding joy that settles upon the heart as our Lord and God reveals himself to us and reveals us to ourselves? As Truman G. Madsen wisely wrote many years ago: "One begins mortality with the veil drawn, but slowly he is moved to penetrate the veil within himself. He is, in time, led to seek the 'holy of holies' within the temple of his own being."[3] Do we grasp what sweet privileges can come to the Saints of the Most High when they slow down, pause, reflect, and listen in their prayers? Inspired prayer entails speaking, listening, conversing, communing. Prayer in the Spirit is an entrance, a passageway, to life in the Spirit.

Chapter 15

NOT ALL PRAYERS ARE ALIKE

On June 27, 2001, Shauna and I were helping our son Jeff prepare the ground at his new home for planting sod. It was a hot and rather humid day (well, humid for Utah), and all of us were eager to get the job done. After working for only fifteen or twenty minutes, I began to feel very uncomfortable. I had difficulty breathing and felt lightheaded, dizzy, and nauseated. Then came a feeling of pressure in my chest that gradually grew into pain. I was keeping track of some of these symptoms when my left arm began to go numb.

At that point I commented to Shauna that I did not feel well and was having trouble getting my breath. She suggested that I go into the shade and take a break. I did so, but by then the sweat was pouring off me and my clothing was drenched, as if I'd been tossed into a river. Shauna commented, "You are really pale. You don't look so good." I replied that I didn't feel so good, either.

Then she asked if I wanted her to call an ambulance.

I thought for a few seconds and said I thought it would be best for her to take me to the hospital in our car, which she did.

The trip to the hospital was miserable. I was in the backseat but could not get comfortable either sitting up or lying down. And then the thought occurred to me that I just might die. I was pretty convinced by then that I was having a heart attack, and the possibility of death seemed realistic. For the first time I felt it might be wise to pray. But my mind and body were so caught up in the physical and emotional trauma associated with cardiac arrest that I couldn't seem to harness my thoughts and get my mind in order. Try as I would, I could only manage to cry out in my mind, "O God, please help me. Please help me." It wasn't much of a prayer, but it was all I could manage at the time.

Obviously I lived through the ordeal, although it took surgery and weeks of rehabilitation for me to recover fully. During the decade since, I have reflected many times on those crucial moments. My cardiologist said that if I had been a minute later, I probably would not have made it. I thank God regularly for sparing my life, for inspiring physicians and nurses, and for answering the prayers of family, friends, and members of my stake. I have never felt even remotely guilty for my inability to offer much of a prayer, for I have sensed that the Lord, knowing the trying conditions, understood my situation and my deepest desires perfectly.

When I think back on my full-time service in the Eastern States Mission, I can identify other great spiritual experiences that were foundational events in my life. My companions and I had some powerful moments pleading with the Lord in behalf of our investigators. We also enjoyed marvelous times as we importuned the heavens for people to teach. We were praying for our brothers and sisters who had been kept from the truth because they knew not where to find it (D&C 123:12), and such wrestlings of the soul proved to be sanctifying and soul-satisfying. There were other times when our days had been long and hard and tiresome, when we came home in the evening, knelt beside our beds, and began to pray. What a surprise it was several hours later, in the middle of the night, to wake up on our knees, stiff and sore. We both felt embarrassed before God, although now it seems to me that if anyone understood, he did.

Some prayers are brief but heartfelt. Others are lengthy, poignant, and soul-stretching.

Jacob wrestled with the Lord for a whole night until he received a blessing (Genesis 32:24).

Enos, grandson of Lehi, went into the forest to hunt beasts but discovered that he was in reality hunting for salvation. "And my soul hungered," he wrote, "and I kneeled down before my Maker, and I cried unto him in mighty prayer and supplication for mine own soul; and all the day long did I cry unto him; yea, and when the night came I did still raise my voice high that it reached the heavens. And there came a voice unto me, saying: Enos, thy sins are forgiven thee, and thou shalt be blessed" (Enos 1:4–5).

Even our Lord and Savior came to know something about prayer that he could not have known before his experience in mortality. In the Garden of Gethsemane the Savior began to feel the loss of his Father's sustaining Spirit: "And being in an agony he prayed more earnestly" (Luke 22:44).

Elder Bruce R. McConkie observed of that singular occasion: "Now here is a marvelous thing. Note it well. The Son of God 'prayed more earnestly'! He who did all things well, whose every word was right, whose every emphasis was proper; he to whom the Father gave his Spirit without measure; he who was the only perfect being ever to walk the dusty paths of planet earth—the Son of God 'prayed more earnestly,' teaching us, his brethren [and sisters], that all prayers, his included, are not alike, and that a greater need calls forth more earnest and faith-filled pleadings before the throne of him to whom the prayers of the saints are a sweet savor."[1]

In modern times, Spencer W. Kimball, then president of the Mount Graham Stake in Safford, Arizona, received a telephone call from President J. Reuben Clark Jr. of the First Presidency, who extended to President Kimball a call to serve as a member of the Quorum of the Twelve Apostles. President Kimball, of course, felt deeply inadequate and set about to receive a complete cleansing of his heart and a confirmation that indeed he had been called of God. The phone call came on July 8, giving him some three months to prepare himself for being sustained in the October 1943 general conference.[2]

At the conference, when he was called upon to speak, then-Elder Kimball said: "I believe the brethren were very kind to me in announcing my appointment when they did so that I might make the necessary adjustments in my business affairs, but perhaps they were more inspired to give me the time that I needed of a long period of purification, for in those long days and weeks I did a great deal of thinking and praying, and fasting and praying. . . .

"I remember reading that Jacob wrestled all night, 'until the breaking of the day' [Genesis 32:24], for a blessing; and I want to tell you that for eighty-five nights I have gone through that experience, wrestling for a blessing. Eighty-five times, the breaking of the day has found me on my knees praying to the Lord to help me and strengthen me and make me equal to this great responsibility that has come to me."[3]

It would be a mistake for us to read of Jacob, Enos, Jesus, or President Kimball and conclude that our prayers should be like theirs. I'm pretty certain that their prayers were not alike. The very fact that Jacob's and Enos's and Jesus' prayers are recorded in scripture suggests that they are unusual, out of the ordinary. Yes, there are times when we are in desperate need of comfort, a blessing, an answer, or a confirmation, and we resolve to remain in the attitude of prayer until we receive some relief, some response. There are other times—most of the time, to be sure—when our prayers are heartfelt, sincere, and earnest, and yet they may not occupy long periods of time or endless soul-searching. Not all lessons are alike. Not all sermons are alike. And surely, not all conversations, including those we enjoy with God, are alike.

Chapter 16

PRAYERS OF GRATITUDE

It is comforting to know that no one is required to walk life's paths alone. Each of us should find great satisfaction and strength in knowing that we do not need to face our challenges, undertake our assignments, or resist temptations through our own unaided efforts. No scriptural invitation is given more frequently than the divine encouragement to ask, to seek, to knock. God has made himself available to all his children. He has offered his Beloved Son in willing sacrifice to make possible a forgiveness of sins and the immortality of the soul. And he has sent his Spirit, the Holy Ghost, to comfort, remind, reveal, teach, confirm, sanctify, and seal. Indeed, consider the sweet implications of the following scriptural promise: "I will go before your face. I will be on your right hand and on your left, and my Spirit shall be in your hearts, and mine angels round about you, to bear you up" (D&C 84:88).

I have never felt a moment's hesitation in asking my Heavenly Father for assistance, for clarity, for wisdom, for strength and willpower. It has never even occurred to me that he would be otherwise engaged, put off, offended, or impatient with my requests. I have never sensed that he wished that I would go away, stop asking questions, cease from troubling him with my problems, or end my endless importuning. Even the kindest and most sensitive mortals will reach their limit, identify the last straw, and eventually cry out, "That's it. I just can't take any more. I'm empty. I have no more to give." Our God is limitless and supremely long-suffering. His strength and power are infinite, and his compassion and empathy never fail. As I understand our relationship to Deity, we can never approach the throne of grace and be unwelcome guests.

And yet there is something superbly beautiful, something spiritually refreshing, about a message to our Maker that is free of requests. Some time ago I was invited to speak twice at a religious conference at which I was the only Latter-day Saint. I was warned that there might be some in attendance who didn't like Mormons, who might choose to engage with me on such matters as women and the priesthood, blacks and the priesthood, or plural marriage. While I was honored to be invited to address the conference, I was also nervous and a bit tentative about being challenged and possibly even attacked. No one knows my limitations better than I do. No one knows the gaps in my knowledge and experience better than I do. And no one knows my inabilities in articulating the truths of the Restoration better than I do. Knowing my weakness, I pleaded long and hard every day for divine comfort and help. I did not want to embarrass the Church or Brigham Young University. Until only moments before my first presentation I could be found in my motel room on my knees.

To make a long but wonderful story short, the conference went magnificently. I have seldom been in a public setting with persons of other faiths when I have been better received, when interest was so high and curiosity was so contagious. The questions were rigorous but appropriate. The people were eager but kind. As the week wore on and as more and more participants at the conference contacted me for my business card and asked if they could communicate with me in the future, my soul was filled with satisfaction. I sensed strongly that the Lord had in fact superintended the occasion and seen to it that a proper impression was made.

On the last morning, with assignments met and sessions attended, I stood in my room, free of pressure, and gazed out my window upon the city. I felt the need to cry out in prayer to my God. I found myself talking aloud in prayer, expressing thanks. It actually didn't feel right to ask for anything. It wasn't as though it would have been wrong to do so, or that my Father in Heaven would have punished me or anything like that. It just seemed like a time for gratitude.

A modern apostle, Elder David A. Bednar, has offered the following pertinent counsel: "The most meaningful and spiritual prayers I have experienced contained many expressions of thanks and few, if any, requests. As I am blessed now to pray with apostles and prophets, I find among these modern-day leaders of the Savior's Church the same characteristic that describes Captain Moroni in the Book of Mormon: these are men whose hearts swell with thanksgiving to God for the many privileges and blessings which he bestows upon his people (see Alma 48:12). . . .

"As we strive to make our prayers more meaningful," Elder Bednar continued, "we should remember that 'in nothing doth man offend God, or against none is his wrath kindled, save those who confess not his hand in all things, and obey not his commandments' (D&C 59:21). Let me recommend that periodically you and I offer a prayer in which we only give thanks and express gratitude. Ask for nothing; simply let our souls rejoice and strive to communicate appreciation with all the energy of our hearts."[1]

My guess is that you and I will never run out of things for which to thank God. We are infinitely blessed, for we are part of a plan of salvation that is infinite and eternal. God showers us with blessings frequently, and we would do well to express extended thanks at least periodically. Undying gratitude is a sign of spiritual maturity, a quiet indication that the Spirit of the Lord is working ever so surely on our hearts, pointing us to our Benefactor, directing our hearts and minds to the ultimate source of satisfaction and security.

Chapter 17

VAIN REPETITIONS

Nobody prays more often than a missionary does. I once tried to keep track of how many times my companion and I offered prayer in a given day, and I was startled to discover that we had prayed together more than fifteen times! Think about it: kneeling personal prayer at 6:30 A.M., companion prayer to begin study class, breakfast prayer, prayer to guide personal study, prayer before leaving the apartment, prayers with people who let us into their homes, prayers with investigators taking the discussions, lunch prayers, dinner prayers, companion prayer at the end of the day, and personal prayer before bed.

Not long after I had tabulated how many times we had lifted our voices heavenward, I was reading the Sermon on the Mount and was sobered by the Savior's warning: "But when ye pray, use not vain repetitions, as the heathen do: for they think that they shall be heard for their much speaking. Be not ye therefore like unto them: for your Father knoweth what things ye have need of, before ye ask him" (Matthew 6:7–8).

I was concerned. Were we guilty of "vain repetitions"? We certainly used "much speaking" to God during the day. Were we offending him? Should we cut back on the number of prayers we offered? As for the matter of repetition, I found myself asking: How many ways are there to ask for the Lord's Spirit to guide us? What different approaches can we take in asking the Lord to bless our investigators? And, perhaps more telling, how much variety can there be in how we ask a blessing on our food? It began to dawn on me that perhaps the problem was not in how many times we prayed but rather in how sincere our prayers were. If what we were saying was not intended to impress anyone, if we were not trying to put on a show, if our deepest desire was to seek divine strength and power in carrying out a labor that was his and not ours—then the Lord was pleased with our petitions.

Vain means empty, shallow, void of substance. Vain repetitions are therefore empty phrases, shallow proclamations. In the Sermon on the Mount, the Lord Jesus calls his followers to a higher righteousness. In Matthew 6 we are cautioned against doing the right things for the wrong reason, against doing good deeds, praying, and fasting to be seen of men rather than God.

Daniel D. McArthur described a dinner at the home of the Prophet Joseph Smith: "When noon came we were all called to dinner at Joseph's house. The table was loaded down with corn-meal mush and milk, and at the bidding of Joseph we all stepped forward to our places around the table, standing on our feet. Joseph asked Joshua Holman, who was one of the wood haulers, to ask a blessing upon the food. He went at his duty with all his soul. As he had been a Methodist exhorter before joining the Church, he commenced to call upon the great and mighty God who sat upon the top of a topless throne, to look down and bless the food and asked many other blessings to rest upon the Prophet, etc.

"As soon as he closed Brother Joseph said, 'Brother Joshua, don't let me ever hear you ask another such blessing;' and then before we took our seats he stated his reasons for making this remark, and showed us how inconsistent such ideas were, and told us many things about God and who He was. Then we sat down to our mush and milk."[1]

I suppose we border on vain repetition when we allow our personal prayers to become rote or ritualistic or almost meaningless. When we rush through our evening prayers, for example, as though they are the final task to be performed before we climb into bed, then those prayers serve little or no function. We would be better off to take a few moments to offer a brief but sincere prayer. Our Lord and Savior knows firsthand what it feels like to be tired; he is no stranger to hunger, thirst, and fatigue (Mosiah 3:7).

But there is little reason to be rushed in our prayers. We just may need to plan our time—including how and when we will pray—a little better in the future. Some have found it helpful, if they plan to stay up later than normal, to retire to their bedside for prayers earlier in the evening while they still have energy and clarity of thought. And frankly, it has always amazed me that Christians who would never consider going to sleep at night without prayer have no problem in rushing off to school or work in the morning without praying. There are so many difficulties and temptations and distractions during the day that I, for one, would feel almost undone, and certainly inadequate, if I had not offered thanks and pleaded for divine help in the morning.

It is inevitable that in many of our conversations with others—perhaps hundreds of hours of talking and listening in a month's time—our attention may slip or our sincerity may slacken. How ironic that we should allow the same thing to happen when we speak to the God of the universe, he who knows all, he who perceives our thoughts and intentions, he whose all-seeing eye penetrates to the core of all things. We cannot fool God, and we should avoid the very appearance of doing so. He deserves our full attention. He is worthy of our focus. He delights when our prayers are from the heart.

Chapter 18

PRAYING FOR OUR ENEMIES

It is so very easy to get into the habit of praying over and over and over again for what we want, for those things that would make our day go better, our problems fade away, our life more pleasant. And we ought to feel perfectly appropriate about asking for the Lord's blessings upon every phase of our lives:

- to become more Christlike in attitudes and behavior,
- to be a more loving father or mother,
- to be a better and more cooperative member of my family,
- to succeed in my education or training to qualify for gainful employment,
- to provide adequately and sufficiently for my family,
- to become a gospel scholar,
- to be worthy and prepared to serve a full-time mission,

- to marry in the temple,
- to have healthy and happy and faith-filled children,
- to love more deeply and thereby become an instrument in the Lord's hands to do good and make a difference more regularly, and
- to endure faithfully to the end of mortality.

On the other hand, what about prayers that petition the Lord for greater popularity? For winning the golf tournament or the Rose Bowl? For that lovely young woman to fall in love with my unmarried son? For my book to hit number one on the New York Times Bestseller list? If we are not careful, we can find ourselves asking for things inappropriately, selfishly—asking amiss, as the scriptures call it (James 4:3; 2 Nephi 4:35). We are instructed in modern revelation that "whatsoever ye ask the Father in my name it shall be given unto you, *that is expedient for you*; and if ye ask anything that is not expedient for you, it shall turn unto your condemnation" (D&C 88:64–65; emphasis added).

In short, we must take care with our prayers and use wisdom and unselfishness in our requests.

Of course it is always proper to pray for ourselves, our families, and our friends. But the Savior challenges us to expand our borders of concern: "Ye have heard that it hath been said, Thou shalt love thy neighbour, and hate thine enemy. But I say unto you, Love your enemies, bless them that curse you, do good to them that hate you, and pray for them which despitefully use you, and persecute you" (Matthew 5:44–45; see also 3 Nephi 12:43–44).

Whoa! That's a different matter entirely. Does Jesus really expect me to pray for those who dislike me or even hate me? Who slander me, who knowingly hurt my reputation? Does he think that I should pray for those who would rather our family had never moved into the neighborhood? Does he believe I should pray for that man who always insults me, even when I try to be kind to him? I can still remember hearing Nikita Krushchev, the premier of the Soviet Union, declare to the people of the United States: "We will bury you." Am I supposed to pray for that kind of person? What about those who continue to state that the Latter-day Saints are members of a cult, that we are not Christian, that we worship a different Jesus and follow a different gospel?

Yes, perplexing and ponderous and painful as it may seem, you and I have been commissioned to stand on higher ground, to turn the other cheek, to forgive and to desire the best for those who hurt us, and even to pray for them. Further, as the Master said, we are to love them! Boy, this Christianity business is tough.

Now I doubt that Christ would want me to pray that the insulting man would stop coming to Church or that the unfriendly neighbors would move from the area. I rather suppose he would not feel good about a prayer from me that all anti-Mormons suddenly go the way of Ananias and Sapphira in the New Testament (Acts 5). And I think our Lord would be quite disappointed if I should ask the

Father to silence my detractors, to strike them dumb, like Korihor (Alma 30:49–50). Generally speaking, God does not honor such requests. Moreover, prayers of that sort are not good for the human heart; rather, they canker the soul. How then do I pray for my enemies?

It would be appropriate to pray that those who seek to harm me or mine will have their anger turned away. It would always be right to pray that those who have a mind to seek our destruction—and do so because of the traditions of men and because they know no better—eventually come to see the error of their ways and have their perspectives broadened and their hearts softened. And perhaps we could pray no more powerful a prayer than to ask a merciful God to bless our enemies that they would cease being our enemies. Zenos, the great prophet of the brass plates, prayed, "Thou art merciful, O God, for thou hast heard my prayer, even when I was in the wilderness; yea, thou wast merciful when I prayed concerning those who were mine enemies, and thou didst turn them to me" (Alma 33:4). Or, as the wise man taught, "When a man's ways please the Lord, he maketh even his enemies to be at peace with him" (Proverbs 16:7). Our Heavenly Father is in the business of reconciliation, and surely nothing could cause the angels in heaven to rejoice more than to witness warring nations or disputing tribes or conflicted individuals coming together once again.

In addition, the more we pray for our enemies, the more our hearts turn toward them. We cannot, in sincerity, continue to lift up in prayer the names of persons

who seek our harm without our being better, without
our own hearts being transformed, our desires and attitudes being altered. It is worth noting that when Alma
and his missionary colleagues discovered the apostasy of
the Zoramites (Alma 31), they were startled and certainly,
as we would say today, turned off. When they witnessed
the Zoramites' near worship of riches, as well as their hy-
pocrisy and self-righteousness on the Rameumptom, their
hearts were grieved. Alma did what seemed proper at the
time—he prayed. He expressed to the Almighty how upset
he and his brethren were to behold the perversion and
"infidelity" of this strange people (v. 30). "O, how long, O
Lord, wilt thou suffer that thy servants shall dwell here
below in the flesh, to behold such gross wickedness among
the children of men?" (v. 26). Later he pleaded, "O Lord,
wilt thou give me strength, that I may bear with mine
infirmities" (v. 30). But then, as the moments passed and
as Alma continued to commune with that all-wise Being
who loves all of his children, Alma's heart was touched:
"Behold, O Lord, their souls are precious, and many of
them are our brethren; therefore, give unto us, O Lord,
power and wisdom that we may bring these, our brethren,
again unto thee" (v. 35).

God and Christ are in the business of people, and
we are called to labor with them. They do not love me
more than they love Buddhists or Hindus or even radi-
cal Islamic Jihaddists. And while I tend to think most
often and feel most fondly about those within my immediate sphere, the call to Christian discipleship is a call to

broaden out, to expand my spiritual horizons, to come to think more often of those I do not know as well and of those I am not as inclined to love and bless and serve, and, yes, to pray for.

Chapter 19

LUKE'S GOSPEL OF PRAYER

Each of the four Gospels in the New Testament demonstrates that Jesus spent a good deal of his time in prayer. He loved his Father. He desired to be constantly in contact with the Almighty and under his heavenly tutelage. Jesus had no private agenda, no secret plan of his own to carry out. Interestingly, the Gospel of Luke includes more accounts of our Master praying than do the other three Gospels.

Mark writes of the baptism of Jesus: "And it came to pass in those days, that Jesus came from Nazareth of Galilee, and was baptized of John in Jordan. And straightway coming up out of the water, he saw the heavens opened, and the Spirit like a dove descending upon him: and there came a voice from heaven, saying, Thou art my beloved Son, in whom I am well pleased" (Mark 1:9–11).

Matthew adds the detail of John's reluctance to baptize the Son of God and of Jesus' response: "Suffer it to be so now: for thus it becometh us to fulfil all righteousness. Then he suffered him" (Matthew 3:15).

Note Luke's unique insertion: "Now when all the people were baptized, it came to pass, that Jesus also being baptized, and praying, the heaven was opened" (Luke 3:21).

What a small but touching detail! Can we picture the sinless Son of Man of Holiness humbling himself before man and God, submitting to the authority of John the Baptist, and then praying during the performance of the ordinance? He who had the power to create worlds without number (Moses 1:33; 7:30), who could command the waves to be still (Mark 4:36–41), multiply a few loaves and fishes to feed five thousand and then four thousand (Matthew 14:15–21; 15:32–38), and command the dead to rise (Luke 7:11–16; John 11:1–44)—this same King of Kings and Lord of Lords felt the need to pray at the time of his baptism.

As recorded in Matthew 8, Mark 1, and Luke 5, Jesus is approached by a leper who cries out, "Lord, if thou wilt, thou canst make me clean. And Jesus put forth his hand, and touched him, saying, I will; be thou clean. And immediately his leprosy was cleansed" (Matthew 8:2–3). Jesus then requested that the man keep the matter to himself, except for meeting with the priest to be declared ritually clean (Matthew 8:2–4). Mark adds that instead, the former leper "went out, and began to publish it much, and to blaze abroad the matter, insomuch that Jesus could no more openly enter into the city" (Mark 1:45). "But so much the more went there a fame abroad of him," Luke writes, "and great multitudes came together to hear, and to be healed by him of their infirmities." Now note this brief sentence: "And he withdrew himself into the wilderness, and prayed" (Luke 5:15–16).

When it came time for Jesus to call and ordain his Twelve Apostles, Matthew writes simply that "when he had called unto him his twelve disciples, he gave them power against unclean spirits, to cast them out, and to heal all manner of sickness and all manner of disease" (Matthew 10:1). The names of the Twelve follow.

Mark states simply that Jesus went "up into a mountain, and calleth unto him whom he would: and they came in unto him. And he ordained twelve, that they should be with him, and that he might send them forth to preach, and to have power to heal sicknesses, and to cast out devils" (Mark 3:13–15).

Luke gives us an important addition: "And it came to pass in those days, that he went out into a mountain to pray, and continued all night in prayer to God. And when it was day, he called unto him his disciples: and of them he chose twelve, whom also he named apostles" (Luke 6:12–13). Luke wants us to understand that only after the Savior had prepared himself through intense and extended prayer did he appoint those who would be sent out as "special witnesses of the name of Christ in all the world" (D&C 107:23).

A powerful scene in the life of the Savior took place at Caesarea Philippi some six months before his atoning sacrifice and crucifixion. There Jesus asked the Twelve,

"Whom do men say that I the Son of man am?" (Matthew 16:13). The answers included John the Baptist (Herod was convinced that Jesus was the martyred Baptist returned to life), Elijah (whose coming had been prophesied by Malachi), Jeremiah (who, like Jesus, had counseled the people of Israel to render obeisance to their political overlords), or another of the prophets.

"But whom say ye that I am?" Jesus followed up. Matthew records that Simon Peter, speaking for all the members of his quorum, boldly and unashamedly proclaimed, "Thou art the Christ, the Son of the living God" (Matthew 16:13–16). According to Mark's account, Peter says, "Thou art the Christ" (Mark 8:29). Luke is the only evangelist to record that "as [Jesus] was *alone praying,* his disciples were with him: and he asked them, saying, Whom say the people that I am?" (Luke 9:18; emphasis added). A week later, Luke explains, the Savior and his chosen servants climb the Mount of Transfiguration "to pray. And as he prayed, the fashion of his countenance was altered, and his raiment was white and glistering" (Luke 9:28–29). This experience sounds very much like the prayer and transfiguration that will take place several months later while Jesus ministers among his American Hebrews, except in the latter case it is Jesus' countenance that shines upon the Nephites as they are praying to him (3 Nephi 19:25–28, 30).

The Savior's ordeal in Gethsemane is mentioned only in the Synoptic Gospels. In each one, in only slightly different language, we get a brief glimpse of the greatest act of love, of mercy and grace, of mediation and intercession, of sacred and sweet surrender, and of reconciliation and atonement, anywhere and anytime in human or salvation history. Having left the upper room after the glorious but melancholy Last Supper, Jesus and the eleven apostles made their way across the Brook Kidron and climbed the Mount of Olives to what was known as the Garden of Gethsemane—the garden of the oil press or garden of the wine press—a place where the Savior "ofttimes resorted thither with his disciples" (John 18:2), a place where he was accustomed to being (Luke 22:39). "There Jesus taught his disciples the doctrines of the kingdom, and all of them communed with Him who is the Father of us all, in whose ministry they were engaged, and on whose errand they served."[1]

Now consider the vital details in Luke's account: "And when he was at the place, he said unto them, Pray that ye enter not into temptation. And he was withdrawn from them [the eleven] about a stone's cast, and kneeled down, and prayed, saying, Father, if thou be willing, remove this cup from me: nevertheless not my will, but thine, be done. And there appeared an angel unto him from heaven, strengthening him. And being in an agony he prayed more earnestly: and his sweat was as it were great drops of blood falling down to the ground" (Luke 22:40–44).

One direct consequence of sin is the withdrawal of the Father's Spirit, resulting in feelings of loss, anxiety, disappointment, fear, alienation, and guilt. Latter-day Saint scripture and prophets affirm that Jesus experienced the withdrawal of the Father's Spirit and thus suffered in body and in spirit, both in the Garden of Gethsemane and on the cross of Calvary (D&C 19:15–20). The withdrawal of the Spirit lasted for a period of hours in Gethsemane and recurred on the cross the next day. It was for this reason that Jesus cried out from the cross, "My God, my God, why hast thou forsaken me?" (Matthew 27:46).

Jacob, son of Lehi, described our Lord's sufferings as follows: "And he cometh into the world that he may save all men if they will hearken unto his voice; for behold, he suffereth the pains of all men, yea, the pains of every living creature, both men, women, and children, who belong to the family of Adam" (2 Nephi 9:21). The difference for Latter-day Saints is their belief that the Savior's suffering in Gethsemane was not just prelude to the Atonement but a vital and important part of it. An angel, speaking to King Benjamin of the coming of the Messiah, said, "And lo, he shall suffer temptations, and pain of body, hunger, thirst, and fatigue, even more than man can suffer, except it be unto death; for behold, blood cometh from every pore, so great shall be his anguish for the wickedness and the abominations of his people" (Mosiah 3:7).

President Brigham Young spoke specifically of what made Jesus sweat blood in the garden: "God never bestows upon His people, or upon an individual, superior blessings without a severe trial to prove them, to prove that individual, or that people. . . . For this express purpose the Father withdrew His spirit from His Son, at the time he was to be crucified. Jesus had been with his Father, talked with Him, dwelt in His bosom, and knew all about heaven, about making the earth, about the transgression of man, and what would redeem the people, and that he was the character who was to redeem the sons of earth, and the earth itself from all sin that had come upon it. The light, knowledge, power, and glory with which he was clothed were far above, or exceeded that of all others who had been upon the earth after the fall, consequently at the very moment, at the hour when the crisis came for him to offer up his life, the Father withdrew Himself, withdrew His Spirit, and cast a vail over him. That is what made him sweat blood. If he had had the power of God upon him, he would not have sweat blood; but all was withdrawn from him, and a veil was cast over him, and he then plead[ed] with the Father not to forsake him."[2]

How this took place we do not know. We believe in Christ and trust in his redeeming mercy and grace. We accept the word of scripture, both ancient and modern, in regard to the ransoming mission of Jesus the Christ. We know from personal experience—having been transformed from pain to peace, from darkness to light—of the power in Christ to renew the human soul. But, like the rest of the Christian world, we cannot rationally comprehend the work of a God. We cannot grasp how one man can assume the effect of another man's error, and, more especially, how one man, even a man possessed of the power of God, can suffer for another's sins. Though real, the Atonement, the greatest act of mercy and love in all eternity, is for now incomprehensible and unfathomable.

Chapter 20

THE RISEN LORD PRAYS

And it came to pass that when they had all been brought, and Jesus stood in the midst, he commanded the multitude [some twenty-five hundred men, women, and children] that they should kneel down upon the ground. And it came to pass that when they had knelt upon the ground, Jesus groaned within himself, and said: Father, I am troubled because of the wickedness of the people of the house of Israel" (3 Nephi 17:13–14).

Here we see the sublime sensitivity and omniscient awareness of our Master. Although the gathered Nephites represented the "more righteous" (3 Nephi 10:12) part of this New World society, Jesus was fully aware of the unrighteous ones who had been destroyed during the upheaval that preceded his visit (3 Nephi 8) and also of the waywardness and wickedness among his people in the Old World. He knew of the inner noise and spiritual discomfort that accompany serious sin. Isaiah had declared some seven centuries earlier that "the wicked are like the troubled sea, when it cannot rest, whose waters cast up mire and dirt. There is no peace, saith my God, to the wicked" (Isaiah 57:20–21; compare 48:22). As Alma taught an errant son, "wickedness never was happiness," and those who are "in a state of nature, or . . . in a carnal state, are in the gall of bitterness and in the bonds of iniquity." Not only are they enemies of God—working at cross purposes to the great plan of happiness—but, tragically, they are also enemies to themselves, laboring against their best good. Again in Alma's words, "they are without God in the world, and they have gone contrary to the nature of God; therefore, they are in a state contrary to the nature of happiness" (Alma 41:10–11).

After Jesus had groaned concerning the wickedness of his covenant people, "he himself also knelt upon the earth; and behold he prayed unto the Father, and the things which he prayed cannot be written, and the multitude did bear record who heard him.

"And after this manner do they bear record: The eye hath never seen, neither hath the ear heard, before, so great and marvelous things as we saw and heard Jesus speak unto the Father;

"And no tongue can speak, neither can there be written by any man, neither can the hearts of men conceive so great and marvelous things as we both saw and heard Jesus speak; and no one can conceive of the joy which filled our souls at the time we heard him pray for us unto the Father" (3 Nephi 17:15–17).

Why could they not be written? Some spiritual

experiences are so specific to time and place, so reserved for the ears and eyes and hearts of those who experience them, that it is simply wrong, divinely inappropriate, to speak openly of them, to try to rehearse or record them. In addition, some matters are ineffable, literally unspeakable or unrecordable. Words fail us. Telestial or even terrestrial expressions cannot do justice to celestial phenomena.

Thus the Prophet Joseph Smith and Sidney Rigdon wrote the following at the end of the vision of the glories, a recitation that was at best a hundredth part of what they saw and experienced[1]:

"Great and marvelous are the works of the Lord, and the mysteries of his kingdom which he showed unto us, which surpass all understanding in glory, and in might, and in dominion;

"Which he commanded us we should not write while we were yet in the Spirit, and are not lawful for man to utter;

"Neither is man capable to make them known, for *they are only to be seen and understood by the power of the Holy Spirit,* which God bestows on those who love him, and purify themselves before him" (D&C 76:114–16; emphasis added).

After the risen Lord's transcendent prayer, he called the little children unto him, one by one, blessed them, and prayed for them (3 Nephi 17:21–24). Jesus was overcome by the experience and wept. Only one who has looked deeply into the eyes of little children can grasp why. Only one who has sensed how near little children are to the heavens, how close to the angels, how innocent and worthy of our respect, admiration, and awe can know why the Purest of the Pure wept as he associated with the purest among the Nephites. Angels came down and ministered to their little ones, an event that bespeaks a mighty truth, one that the Lord had taught in the Old World:

"Take heed that ye despise not one of these little ones; for I say unto you, That in heaven their angels [premortal spirits²] do always behold the face of my Father which is in heaven" (Matthew 18:10). Indeed, how we feel toward little children, how we treat them, how we speak to them—these are fairly good measures of how much like the Master we are.

An important question, just beneath the surface of most conversations about prayer, that yearns to be addressed is, Why did Jesus need to pray?

To begin with, during his mortal ministry he set aside much of the power and glory he had enjoyed before he came into the world (John 17:5). Paul wrote that Jesus "made himself of no reputation, and took upon him the form of a servant, and was made in the likeness of men: and being found in fashion as a man, he humbled himself, and became obedient unto death, even the death of the cross" (Philippians 2:7–8). Other translations render this passage as "emptied himself, taking the form of a slave" (New American Bible; see also New Revised Standard Version). By choice Jesus refrained from turning the stones to bread, although he certainly possessed the power to do so (Luke 4:3–4). By choice Jesus refrained from casting himself down from the pinnacle of the temple and anticipating divine deliverance, although he had the power to do so (Luke 4:9–12). By choice our Lord refrained from calling down legions of angels to deliver him in the Garden of Gethsemane, although he indeed possessed the power to do so (Matthew 26:51–54). And by choice the Master of ocean and earth and skies refrained from descending from the cross and ending the pain and suffering, the ignominy and irony of his crucifixion and death, although he had the power to do just that (Matthew 27:39–40; Luke 23:39).

By setting aside power and glory, he was able to know mortality in its fulness, to know by experience what it felt like to be hungry, thirsty, tired, snubbed, ridiculed, excluded. In short, he chose to endure the throes and toils of this estate so that he could know how to succor his people (Alma 7:11–13; D&C 62:1). Thus, when he felt the need for reassurance, he prayed to his Father in Heaven. When he needed answers or perspective, he prayed. When he needed the sacred sustaining influence of the Father in his darkest hours, he prayed. Because of the Spirit, which conveys the mind of God (1 Corinthians 2:16), he was in the Father, as the Father was in him. They were one.[3]

Then what of the risen Lord praying among the Nephites? Why would a glorified, immortal, and resurrected being, now possessing the fulness of the glory and power of the Father (Matthew 28:18; D&C 93:16), spend so much of his time in prayer among the Nephites? Was there some truth he did not know, some godly attribute he did not possess, some energy or strength he lacked? Was there some approval of the Father, some encouragement or permission, he needed? I rather think not. The descendants of Lehi might have cried out *Emmanuel,* "God is with us." Obviously, the Savior prayed as an example to all people of the need to communicate with God—often, regularly, consistently, intensely, reverently.

Building on these truths, we therefore ask, further, are there not other purposes of prayer, both in time and in eternity? Jesus prayed to the Father because he loved the Father. Jesus prayed to the Father because prayer was a reverential way of speaking to his Father, who is forever worthy of the reverence of his children. Jesus prayed to the Father because they enjoyed communion. The word *communion* is an especially meaningful word, one that is worth much reflection, a word that means "to be with." Jesus possessed perfect spirituality because he had overcome the world (John 16:33; D&C 101:36) and because he enjoyed perfect communion with the Father.

This pattern of prayer, this communion, is a call to you and to me to live our lives in such a manner that we cultivate more fully the cleansing and revelatory benefits of the Spirit; that we yield our hearts to God (Helaman 3:35) and have an eye single to his glory (D&C 88:67); that we allow our conscience to be strengthened, our judgment to be refined, and our desires to be educated. Through such communion with God we will become bearers of the fruit of the Spirit—charity, or the pure love of Christ—so that this grandest of all spiritual gifts and graces will reign triumphantly in our speech and actions and attitudes, and thus, eventually, we will have become like our God and thereby be able to see him as he is (Galatians 5:22–25; 1 John 3:1–3; Moroni 7:45–48).

All of this points us to the relationship between the Father and the Son. The truth is that even though Jesus possessed the fulness of the glory and power of the Father, possessed the same divinity with the Father, yet he still looked to the Father as his superior. It would never seem appropriate, for example, for the Father to pray to the Son or the Holy Ghost. In the words of Elder Parley P. Pratt, Christ "differs in nothing from his Father except in age and authority, the Father having the seniority and, consequently, the right, according to the patriarchal laws of eternal priesthood, to preside over him and over all his dominions, for ever and ever. . . .

"The difference between Jesus Christ and his Father is this: one is subordinate to the other and does nothing of himself independently of the Father, but does all things in the name and by the authority of the Father, being of the same mind in all things." Elder Pratt further explained how exalted men and women relate to the Godhead: "The difference between Jesus Christ and another immortal and celestial man is this: the man is subordinate to Jesus Christ and does nothing in and of himself, but does all things in the name of Christ and by his authority, being of the same mind and ascribing all the glory to him and his Father."[4]

"Jesus valued prayer enough to spend many hours at

the task," Christian scholar Philip Yancey wrote. "If I had to answer the question, 'Why pray?' in one sentence, it would be, 'Because Jesus did.' He bridged the chasm between God and human beings. While on earth he became vulnerable, as we are vulnerable, rejected, as we are rejected, and tested, as we are tested. In every case his response was prayer."[5]

Jesus Christ is truly the Light we hold up to one another and to all the world (3 Nephi 18:24). Mere mortals are but dim reflections of that light, mere lamps as compared to the light of the Son. In prayer, as in all facets of our lives, we look to our Model and Master: "And as I have prayed among you even so shall ye pray in my church. . . . Behold I am the light; I have set an example for you" (3 Nephi 18:16).

We seek to follow and emulate the praying Savior.

Chapter 21

GOD SPEED THE RIGHT

We live in challenging times. Pornography and perversion of every kind spread throughout the earth. Wickedness in high places, greed and deception in business and personal dealings, the dissolution of the nuclear family, and the erosion of moral values—these bespeak the seriousness of the secular slouch that our world is undergoing. In that context and not long ago, President Boyd K. Packer delivered this sobering message: "I charge each of you . . . and put you on alert: These are days of great spiritual danger for this people. The world is spiraling downward at an ever-quickening pace. I am sorry to tell you that it will not get better.

"I know of nothing in the history of the Church or in the history of the world to compare with our present circumstances. Nothing happened in Sodom and Gomorrah which exceeds the wickedness and depravity which surrounds us now."[1]

President Gordon B. Hinckley likewise stated: "No

one need tell you that we are living in a very difficult season in the history of the world. Standards are dropping
everywhere. Nothing seems to be sacred any more.

"... The traditional family is under heavy attack.
*I do not know that things were worse in the times of Sodom
and Gomorrah.* At that season, Abraham bargained with
the Lord to save these cities for the sake of the righteous. Notwithstanding his pleas, things were so bad that
Jehovah decreed their destruction. They and their wicked
inhabitants were annihilated. We see similar conditions
today. They prevail all across the world. I think our Father
must weep as He looks down upon His wayward sons and
daughters.

"In the Church we are working very hard to stem the
tide of this evil. But it is an uphill battle."[2]

There has never been a time when the light and love
and leavening influence of the Saints of the Most High
God were needed more than they are today. Many of us
tremble as we realize that the voice of the people is beginning to choose that which is wrong (Mosiah 29:26–27). We
look with soberness at a world that has begun to marginal-
ize, ignore, and even silence the voices of faithful disciples
of the Lord Jesus Christ. The scene is hauntingly familiar.
Truly, "if it were not for the prayers of the righteous, who
are now in the land, that ye would even now be visited
with utter destruction. . . . But it is by the prayers of the
righteous that ye are spared; now therefore, if ye will cast
out the righteous from among you then will not the Lord

stay his hand; but in his fierce anger he will come out against you" (Alma 10:22–23; compare Helaman 13:12).

Can we turn things around? Can this nation and the nations of the earth be spared the fate of civilizations past who rejected the God of all creation and chose the lowest common denominator of existence? I do not know. But I do know that we must work and labor and pray as though a lasting change could come. I am reminded of the words of Mormon to his son Moroni at the stunning close of the Nephite civilization. Mormon spoke of the degraded status of his people, such that they had no fear of death and no love for one another. Further, they had begun to thirst for blood and revenge. Note these poignant words of Mormon: "And now, my beloved son, notwithstanding their hardness, let us labor diligently; for if we should cease to labor, we should be brought under condemnation; for we have a labor to perform whilst in this tabernacle of clay, that we may conquer the enemy of all righteousness, and rest our souls in the kingdom of God" (Moroni 9:6).

We who have been sent to earth at this time, charged to be the savor of men and thus their saviors (D&C 103:9–10), have no choice—we must work and labor to keep ourselves unspotted from the sins and vices of the world. And we must pray. Oh, how we must pray! We must pray with all the energy we possess, both that we may be free from taint and that we may have the power of God in our lives sufficient to make a difference in a world that desperately needs to be diverted from its destructive course.

Few things could have a more powerful effect on a

wicked world than the continuing spread of the gospel of Jesus Christ. "In view of all that prevails in the world," Elder Bruce R. McConkie declared, "it might be easy to center our attention on negative or evil things, or to dissipate our energies on causes and enterprises of doubtful worth and questionable productivity.

"I am fully aware of the divine decree to be actively engaged in a good cause; of the fact that every true principle which works for the freedom and blessing of mankind has the Lord's approval; of the need to sustain and support those who espouse proper causes and advocate true principles—all of which things we also should do in the best and most beneficial way we can. The issue, I think, is not *what* we should do but *how* we should do it; and I maintain that *the most beneficial and productive thing which Latter-day Saints can do to strengthen every good and proper cause is to live and teach the principles of the everlasting gospel.*"[3]

The gospel is the power of God unto salvation (Romans 1:16). It is that sacred system that our Heavenly Father has ordained, with Jesus Christ at its center, for the banishment of evil influences, the cultivation of virtue, the promulgation of decency and nobility, the transformation of human nature and character, and the renovation of society from the inside out. There is no power on earth like it. It is a system of change and divine development that has no peer. You and I must pray for its spread—for God to raise up even more messengers to match our message; for the walls within people's minds and hearts, as well as the walls that prevent whole nations from basking in the light of supernal truth, to come down; for conversion and courage and conviction to fill our hearts and motivate us to identify friends and neighbors and associates and family members who could and should hear the message of salvation; for wards and stakes of Zion, together with holy temples, to dot the earth and bring the full blessings of exaltation to all of our Father's children.

As we observed earlier, "the effectual fervent prayer of a righteous man [or woman] availeth much" (James 5:16). The Church of Jesus Christ needs effectual, fervent prayers. This world needs men and women of great faith—prayer warriors, if you will—who storm the gates of heaven with their petitions and thereby call down heaven's precious blessings upon our world.

My heart resonates with the plea of President Boyd K. Packer to the Latter-day Saints:

"Learn to pray. Pray often. Pray in your mind, in your heart. Pray on your knees. Prayer is your personal key to heaven. The lock is on your side of the veil."[4]

We sing and we pray:

> Now to heav'n our prayer ascending,
> God speed the right;
> In a noble cause contending,
> God speed the right.
> Be our zeal in heav'n recorded,
> With success on earth rewarded.
> God speed the right. God speed the right.

Be that prayer again repeated,
God speed the right;
Ne'er despairing, though defeated,
God speed the right.
Like the great and good in story,
If we fail, we fail with glory.
God speed the right. God speed the right.

Patient, firm, and persevering, God speed the right;
No event nor danger fearing, God speed the right.
Pains, nor toils, nor trials heeding,
And in heav'n's good time succeeding,
God speed the right. God speed the right.[5]

We pray for the establishment of Zion. We pray for the kingdom of heaven to come and to join with the kingdom of God on earth (D&C 65:5–6). We pray that our Lord and Savior will hasten the time of his coming in glory, to bring to pass a day of millennial splendor, a lengthy season of rest and peace and consummate righteousness.

Conclusion

PRAY ALWAYS

When I first outlined this book you are holding in your hands, I envisioned having fifty chapters. I anticipated devoting six or seven pages to each chapter and thus producing a work of more than three hundred pages. I had made an extensive search of what the scriptures taught on prayer, and I believed that such a vital topic was more than worthy of even a thousand pages. Gradually, however, and through the process of writing, I perceived that less would probably be more. I am now persuaded that the few impressions, brief glimpses, and moments of inspiration I have shared here will do more good than a comprehensive treatment of this singularly significant spiritual discipline.

So where have we been? And what have we learned? Consider the following:

1. Sometimes we pray because that is all we can do or know how to do at the time.

2. We should not attempt to rush into the divine presence. Preparation precedes power in prayer.

3. Jesus set forth in the Lord's Prayer a pattern that teaches us what we ought to do and what we ought to say when we lift our voices heavenward.

4. We have been instructed to pray to our Heavenly Father in the name of his beloved Son, Jesus Christ. His is the only name under heaven by which salvation comes.

5. Although God knows all things (and there is nothing that he does not know), we have been charged to communicate our hopes, dreams, sins, and resolutions to him in prayer.

6. We have every right to believe that God will hear our prayers, that answers can and will come to us, and that we can exercise confidence in this marvelous medium of communication.

7. Answers to prayer come in many and varied forms—through feelings, thoughts, and desires, and especially through sensitive and caring individuals.

8. Not all answers to prayer come immediately or even soon after our petitions have been voiced. Nor are some answers as discernible as others. We are told to importune the Lord, to seek and study and pray for guidance. If after a season of seeking we are still unsure, we have been counseled to act prayerfully according to our best judgment and leave the matter with God.

9. Some blessings, including some answers to prayer, come only through combining sincere prayer with fasting. Fasting and prayer are rejoicing and prayer.

10. Like any other practice, including physical exercise, sometimes we will be eager to pray and at other times less so. When we do not feel like praying, we must pray anyway. Such discipline leads to competent and dedicated discipleship.

11. We need to be cautious about what we say in prayer, especially what we ask for. We just may get it.

12. Much of the time God will answer our prayers through those about us in this world; at other times he will extend help from beyond the veil.

13. If we are careful to avoid praying amiss, the Lord of glory, who delights to honor those who serve him faithfully, will gladly hear our cry and grant our requests.

14. Praying "thy will be done" and meaning it require us to surrender our will to the Father. That surrender is extremely difficult; accomplishing it requires the strength and grace of God.

15. We don't always know what is in our best interest and therefore what we really should pray for. To prompt and inspire the words we should speak in prayer is the work of the Holy Spirit.

16. To some extent every prayer is different, largely because we are different. Some life circumstances may call forth prayers that are sincere but brief; others may require extended expressions of the soul in prayer. We must be spiritually versatile.

17. We must forever be engaged in expressing gratitude and thanks to our benevolent Father, especially in prayer.

18. Rewarding prayer is more than ritual and

repetition. It is heartfelt, substantive, the very doorway to pure religion.

19. Jesus taught us to love and pray for our enemies, for those who despise us, persecute us, and despitefully use us. Such prayers, when prompted and empowered by the Holy Ghost, are soul-stirring and sanctifying.

20. Our Master taught us to pray by praying. He epitomized what you and I should do and be as he sought for and enjoyed constant and continuing communion with his Eternal Father.

21. As wickedness and malevolence increase in today's world, and as we anticipate the depths to which society will descend through giving heed to the father of lies, there is precious little we can do that will be more effective and influential than pleading and persisting in prayer. This world needs our prayers. The people of planet Earth may well be spared by the effectual, fervent prayers of those who care deeply for them. We can do all else that we can to turn things around—legislation, campaigns, and, of course, preaching the gospel of Jesus Christ—but in the end we can and should and must pray that righteousness will spread its wings and evil will be defeated.

Nephi offered sound and solid counsel: "Ye must pray always, and not faint; . . . ye must not perform any thing unto the Lord save in the first place ye shall pray unto the Father in the name of Christ, that he will consecrate thy performance unto thee, that thy performance may be for the welfare of thy soul" (2 Nephi 32:9).

And it may be that Amulek offered one of the finest

descriptions of what it means to pray always when he implored: "Yea, cry unto [God] for mercy; for he is mighty to save. Yea, humble yourselves, and continue in prayer unto him. . . . Cry unto him in your houses, yea, over all your household, both morning, mid-day, and evening. Yea, cry unto him against the power of your enemies. Yea, cry unto him against the devil, who is an enemy to all righteousness. . . . But this is not all; ye must pour out your souls in your closets, and your secret places, and in your wilderness." Now here's the key: "Yea, and when you do not cry unto the Lord, let your hearts be full, drawn out in prayer unto him continually for your welfare, and also for the welfare of those who are around you" (Alma 34:18–19, 21–23, 26–27).

Amulek spoke of how to be engaged in what Elder David A. Bednar has called "meaningful prayer," namely, not only expressing but doing.[1] "After ye have done all these things"—praying wherever and for whatever we need, including the care of the less fortunate—"if ye turn away the needy, and the naked, and visit not the sick and afflicted, and impart of your substance, if ye have, to those who stand in need—I say unto you, if ye do not [do] any of these things, behold, your prayer is vain, and availeth you nothing, and ye are as hypocrites who do deny the faith. Therefore, if ye do not remember to be charitable, ye are as dross, which the refiners do cast out, (it being of no worth) and is trodden under foot of men" (Alma 34:28–29).

Amulek's missionary companion, Alma, likewise

implored: "Yea, and cry unto God for all thy support; yea, let all thy doings be unto the Lord, and whithersoever thou goest let it be in the Lord; yea, let all thy thoughts be directed unto the Lord; yea, let the affections of thy heart be placed upon the Lord forever. Counsel with the Lord in all thy doings, and he will direct thee for good; yea, when thou liest down at night lie down unto the Lord, that he may watch over you in your sleep; and when thou risest in the morning let thy heart be full of thanks unto God; and if ye do these things, ye shall be lifted up at the last day" (Alma 37:36–37; compare Proverbs 3:5–6).

In other words, constant counseling with our Heavenly Father leads to eternal life. Complete reliance upon our Lord and Savior produces faith unto life and salvation.

We must, absolutely must, make time for prayer. We have heard repeated hundreds of times the marvelous directive, "Be still, and know that I am God" (Psalm 46:10). When we understand that *vacate* is a form of the Latin verb meaning "be still," we can understand more fully what scholar Simon Tugwell meant when he said, "God invites us to take a holiday [vacation], to stop being God for a while, and let him be God."[2]

President Dieter F. Uchtdorf observed: "One of the greatest blessings and privileges and opportunities we have as children of our Heavenly Father is that we can communicate with Him. We can speak to Him of our life experiences, trials, and blessings. We can listen for and receive celestial guidance from the Holy Spirit. We can offer our petitions to heaven and receive an assurance that our prayers have been heard and that He will answer them as a loving and wise Father."[3]

I bear witness that God our Father lives, that he is the Father of the spirits of all humankind (Numbers 16:22; 27:16; Hebrews 12:9). He is all-loving, all-powerful, all-knowing, and, by the power of his Spirit, everywhere present. He knows us by name. He knows our thoughts, our feelings, and our soul's deepest longings. He yearns to extend his tender mercies. He hears our prayers, and he answers them.

I further testify of the efficacy of prayer. Prayer has been my source of solace, my avenue of peace, my quiet exit into serenity for a long, long time. There has never been a time in my life when I did not know how significant and how needful it was to pray, how beneficial it was to pray. I know that my very salvation and eternal life depend upon my ability to enjoy sweet communion with my Maker and my blessed Savior. Prayer saves souls. Prayer secures us in the faith. Prayer fortifies us against the cunning and the snares of the devil. Prayer opens us to insights from a higher realm of reality. Prayer transforms us into holy people. Persistent prayer is potent. We never stand taller than when we are on our knees.

I pray, therefore, that our Father in Heaven will grant unto us the peace that passes all understanding (Philippians 4:7), that our lives will be rich and rewarding as a result of our constant attention to prayer, and that one day, before too very long, we may find ourselves "clasped in the arms of Jesus" (Mormon 5:11). Like Nephi, "I pray the Father in the name of Christ that many of us, if not all, may be saved in his kingdom at that great and last day" (2 Nephi 33:12). Indeed, God grant that it may be so.

NOTES

Introduction: Did You Think to Pray?

1. Monson, "Prayer of Faith," 2–4.
2. Stott, *Authentic Christianity*, 225–26.
3. See Yancey, *Prayer*, 13.
4. Stott, *Authentic Christianity*, 226.
5. Hales, "Christian Courage," 72.
6. Kierkegaard, *Purity of Heart*.
7. McKnight, *Jesus Creed*, 17.
8. Graham, *Just As I Am*, 723–24; emphasis added.

Chapter 2: The Lord's Prayer

1. Bonhoeffer, *Cost of Discipleship*, 165.
2. McLaren, *Secret Message of Jesus*, 17.
3. Peterson, *Message*, 1754.

Chapter 3: In the Name of the Son

1. Lewis, *Mere Christianity*, 59.

Notes

Chapter 4: If God Knows All

1. Smith, *Lectures on Faith*, 4.11; 7.15.
2. See also Smith, *Doctrines of Salvation*, 2:269; McConkie, *Mormon Doctrine*, 364.

Chapter 6: Answers to Prayer

1. Smith, *Teachings of the Prophet Joseph Smith*, 151.
2. Hales, "Holy Scriptures," 26–27.
3. Packer, *"That All May Be Edified,"* 335.
4. Monson, "Be Your Best Self," 68.

Chapter 7: When No Clear Answer Comes

1. Smith, *Gospel Doctrine*, 61, 466.
2. Young, *Journal of Discourses*, 3:205.
3. Smith, *Teachings of the Prophet Joseph Smith*, 149.
4. Uchtdorf, "Prayer and the Blue Horizon," 6.
5. Smith, *Teachings of the Prophet Joseph Smith*, 160.
6. "Lead, Kindly Light," *Hymns*, no. 97.

Chapter 8: Fasting and Prayer

1. McKay, *Gospel Ideals*, 390.
2. See Smith, *Lectures on Faith*, 6.1–7.

Chapter 9: When We Don't Feel like Praying

1. Smith, *Biography and Family Record of Lorenzo Snow*, 7–9; paragraphing altered.
2. Young, *Journal of Discourses*, 13:155.
3. Young, *Journal of Discourses*, 7:164.

Chapter 10: Our Words Matter

1. Oaks, *Pure in Heart*, 151.
2. See Packer, "Teach the Children," 15.

Notes

CHAPTER 11: HELP FROM THOSE ON THE OTHER SIDE

1. Smith, Conference Report, April 1916, 2–3; paragraphing altered; see also Clark, *Messages of the First Presidency*, 5:6–7.
2. Smith, *Teachings of George Albert Smith*, 27.
3. Nelson, "Salvation and Exaltation," 10; see also "Celestial Marriage," 92.

CHAPTER 13: SURRENDER IN PRAYER

1. Stanley, *Blessings of Brokenness*, 36–37; emphasis in original.
2. Packer, "Spiritual Crocodiles," 32; emphasis in original.
3. Maxwell, "Swallowed Up in the Will of the Father," 24.
4. Lewis, *Letters to Malcolm*, 25–26.

CHAPTER 14: PRAYER IN SPIRIT

1. Smith, *Teachings of the Prophet Joseph Smith*, 278.
2. In their midst now is the Lord Omnipotent, the great Jehovah, the Promised Messiah, the God of Abraham, Isaac, and Jacob. In their midst is God the Second, the Redeemer (see Smith, *Teachings of the Prophet Joseph Smith*, 190), the God who ministered to Enoch and Noah and who gave the Law to Moses, the one through whom all revelation since the Fall had come. In their midst is the Being the Prophet Joseph Smith termed the Prototype of salvation, the standard of all saved beings (Smith, *Lectures on Faith*, 7.9), a resurrected, immortal, glorified Personage. Would we not be driven by our inner sense of love and divine propriety to worship him? Would we not be enticed, even motivated, to pray to him? Jesus left their midst for a short time, bowed himself to the earth, and prayed. He thanked God the Father for sending the Holy Ghost, saying that "they pray unto me because I am with them" (3 Nephi 19:22). "Jesus was present before them as the symbol of the Father," Elder Bruce R. McConkie

explained. "Seeing him, it was as though they saw the Father [compare John 14:9]; praying to him, it was as though they prayed to the Father. It was a special and unique situation" (*Promised Messiah*, 561).

3. Madsen, *Eternal Man*, 20.

Chapter 15: Not All Prayers Are Alike

1. McConkie, "Why the Lord Ordained Prayer," in *Prayer*, 8.
2. See Kimball and Kimball, *Spencer W. Kimball*, 187–205.
3. Kimball, in Conference Report, October 1943, 15–16.

Chapter 16: Prayers of Gratitude

1. Bednar, "Pray Always," 43.

Chapter 17: Vain Repetitions

1. "Recollections of the Prophet Joseph Smith," 129, cited in Andrus and Andrus, *They Knew the Prophet*, 73–74.

Chapter 19: Luke's Gospel of Prayer

1. McConkie, "Purifying Power of Gethsemane," 9.
2. Young, *Journal of Discourses*, 3:205–6.

Chapter 20: The Risen Lord Prays

1. See Smith, *Teachings of the Prophet Joseph Smith*, 305.
2. See McConkie, *Doctrinal New Testament Commentary*, 1:421.
3. See Smith, *Lectures on Faith*, 5.2.
4. Pratt, *Key to the Science of Theology*, 20–21; see also Smith, *Teachings of the Prophet Joseph Smith*, 347–48.
5. Yancey, *Prayer*, 50.

Chapter 21: God Speed the Right

1. Packer, "On the Shoulders of Giants," 9.

2. Hinckley, "Standing Strong and Immovable," 20; emphasis added.
3. McConkie, "Think on These Things," 46–47; emphasis added.
4. Packer, "Prayer and Promptings," 46.
5. "God Speed the Right," *Hymns*, no. 106.

CONCLUSION: PRAY ALWAYS

1. Bednar, "Ask in Faith," 94.
2. Cited in Yancey, *Prayer*, 26.
3. Uchtdorf, "Prayer and the Blue Horizon," 6.

SOURCES

Andrus, Hyrum L., and Helen Mae Andrus. *They Knew the Prophet*. Salt Lake City: Bookcraft, 1974.

Bednar, David A. "Ask in Faith." *Ensign*, May 2008, 94–97.

———. "Pray Always." *Ensign*, November 2008, 41–44.

Bonhoeffer, Dietrich. *The Cost of Discipleship*. New York: Simon and Schuster, Touchstone, 1995.

Graham, Billy. *Just As I Am: The Autobiography of Billy Graham*. New York: HarperSanFrancisco/Zondervan, 1997.

Hales, Robert D. "Christian Courage: The Price of Discipleship." *Ensign*, November 2008, 72–75.

———. "Holy Scriptures: The Power of God unto Our Salvation." *Ensign*, November 2006, 24–27.

Hinckley, Gordon B. "Standing Strong and Immovable." In *Worldwide Leadership Training Meeting: The Priesthood and the Auxiliaries of the Relief Society, Young Women, and Primary*. Broadcast 10 January 2004. Salt Lake City: The Church of Jesus Christ of Latter-day Saints, 2004. Available online at www.lds.org/broadcast/archive/wwlt/WLTM_2004_01___24240_000.pdf.

Hymns of The Church of Jesus Christ of Latter-day Saints. Salt Lake City: The Church of Jesus Christ of Latter-day Saints, 1985.

Journal of Discourses. 26 vols. Liverpool: F. D. Richards & Sons, 1851–86.

Kierkegaard, Soren. *Purity of Heart Is to Will One Thing: Spiritual Preparation for the Office of Confession.* Translated by Douglas V. Steere. New York: Harper Torchbooks, 1956.

Kimball, Edward L., and Andrew E. Kimball Jr. *Spencer W. Kimball: Twelfth President of The Church of Jesus Christ of Latter-day Saints.* Salt Lake City: Bookcraft, 1977.

Kimball, Spencer W. In Conference Report, October 1943, 15–19.

Lewis, C. S. *Letters to Malcolm: Chiefly on Prayer.* New York: Harcourt Brace and Co., 1992.

———. *Mere Christianity.* New York: Touchstone, 1996.

Madsen, Truman G. *Eternal Man.* Salt Lake City: Deseret Book, 1966.

Maxwell, Neal A. "Swallowed Up in the Will of the Father." *Ensign,* November 1995, 22–24.

McConkie, Bruce R. *Doctrinal New Testament Commentary.* 3 vols. Salt Lake City: Bookcraft, 1965–73.

———. *Mormon Doctrine.* 2d ed. Salt Lake City: Bookcraft, 1966.

———. *The Promised Messiah: The First Coming of Christ.* Salt Lake City: Deseret Book, 1978.

———. "The Purifying Power of Gethsemane." *Ensign,* May 1985, 9–11.

———. "Think on These Things." *Ensign,* January 1974, 45–48.

McKay, David O. *Gospel Ideals.* Salt Lake City: Improvement Era, 1953.

Sources

McKnight, Scot. *The Jesus Creed: Loving God, Loving Others*. Brewster, Mass.: Paraclete Press, 2004.

McLaren, Brian D. *The Secret Message of Jesus: Uncovering the Truth that Could Change Everything*. Nashville: Thomas Nelson, 2006.

Messages of the First Presidency of The Church of Jesus Christ of Latter-day Saints. 6 vols. Edited by James R. Clark. Salt Lake City: Bookcraft, 1965–75.

Monson, Thomas S. "Be Your Best Self." *Ensign*, May 2009, 67–70.

———. "The Prayer of Faith." *Ensign*, August 1995, 2–6.

Nelson, Russell M. "Celestial Marriage." *Ensign*, November 2008, 92–95.

———. "Salvation and Exaltation." *Ensign*, May 2008, 7–10.

Oaks, Dallin H. *Pure in Heart*. Salt Lake City: Bookcraft, 1988.

Packer, Boyd K. "On the Shoulders of Giants." J. Reuben Clark Law Society devotional, Salt Lake City, Utah, 28 February 2004. *Clark Memorandum* (Fall 2004): 2–11. Available online at www.jrcls.org/publications/clark_memo/issues/cmF04.pdf.

———. "Prayer and Promptings." *Ensign*, November 2009, 43–46.

———. "Spiritual Crocodiles." *Ensign*, May 1976, 30–32.

———. "Teach the Children." *Ensign*, February 2000, 10–17.

———. "That All May Be Edified." Salt Lake City: Bookcraft, 1982.

Peterson, Eugene H. *The Message: The Bible in Contemporary Language*. Colorado Springs, Colo.: Nav Press, 2002.

Pratt, Parley P. *Key to the Science of Theology*. Salt Lake City: Deseret Book, 1978.

Prayer. Salt Lake City: Deseret Book, 1977.

Sources

"Recollections of the Prophet Joseph Smith." *Juvenile Instructor* 27 (February 15, 1892): 127–29.

Smith, Eliza R. Snow. *Biography and Family Record of Lorenzo Snow*. Salt Lake City: Deseret News, 1884.

Smith, George Albert. *The Teachings of George Albert Smith*. Edited by Robert and Susan McIntosh. Salt Lake City: Bookcraft, 1996.

Smith, Joseph. *Lectures on Faith*. Salt Lake City: Deseret Book, 1985.

———. *Teachings of the Prophet Joseph Smith*. Selected by Joseph Fielding Smith. Salt Lake City: Deseret Book, 1976.

Smith, Joseph F. Conference Report, April 1916, 1–8.

———. *Gospel Doctrine*. Salt Lake City: Deseret Book, 1971.

Smith, Joseph Fielding. *Doctrines of Salvation*. 3 vols. Compiled by Bruce R. McConkie. Salt Lake City: Bookcraft, 1954–56.

Stanley, Charles. *The Blessings of Brokenness: Why God Allows Us to Go through Hard Times*. Grand Rapids, Michigan: Zondervan, 1997.

Stott, John R. W. *Authentic Christianity from the Writings of John Stott*. Compiled by Timothy Dudley-Smith. Downers Grove, Ill.: InterVarsity Press, 1995.

Uchtdorf, Dieter F. "Prayer and the Blue Horizon." *Ensign*, June 2009, 5–7.

Yancey, Philip. *Prayer: Does It Make Any Difference?* Grand Rapids, Mich.: Zondervan, 2006.

INDEX

Index

into temptation," 21; "For thine is the kingdom," 22; as pattern for us, 127

Love, our enemies, 101

Madsen, Truman G., 84

Marsh, Thomas B., 38

Maxwell, Neal A., 78

McArthur, Daniel D., 96–97

McConkie, Bruce R.: on Jesus praying more earnestly, 89; on preaching the gospel, 123

McKay, David O., 51

McKnight, Scot, 7

Miracle(s): more, if more prayers offered, 4; of prayer, 8; wrought through prayer, 41; worked by fasting and prayer, 52

Missionary experiences, 87–88, 95, 123

Monson, Thomas S.: on praying to be guided, 4; on miracles wrought through prayer, 41

Music, to prepare for prayer, 13

Nelson, Russell M., 70

Oaks, Dallin H., 59

Obstacles, to prayer, 6

Offerings, honesty in paying, 78

Packer, Boyd K.: on answers being a voice one feels, 40; on surrendering agency to God, 77; on world being in great spiritual danger, 120; on prayer as personal key to heaven, 124

Peterson, Eugene, 22

Plight, spiritual, 23

Power, in Jesus Christ's name, 27

Powers of heaven, 50

Pratt, Parley P., 118

Pray: need to, 5; out of desperation, 5; story of book warning others not to, 33–34; Satan teaches not to, 34–35; our right to, 35; duty to, 58; for needs, 83; Holy Ghost teaches us for what we should, 83, 128; why, 115, 119; why Jesus Christ needed to, 115

Prayer(s): for enemies, 2, 101–102, 129; transforms us, 3–5, 132; obstacles to, 6; miracle of, 8; song of the heart is, 13; to prepare for what is to come, 15; lifeline to divine knowledge and power, 32; heard by God, 36; makes a difference, 55; for financial assistance, 74; words for, will be given to us, 75; as communion with Deity, 81–82; made perfect by Holy Ghost, 81; uttered about our needs, 83; major avenue of revelation, 84; for help only, 86–87; on behalf of others, 88; not all alike, 90; rushing through, 97; planning time for, 97–98; cannot fool God, 98; of Jesus, 105–9; is understood by Holy Ghost, 114; makes a difference, 121–22; is all we can do, 125; when we don't feel like it,

Index